The Chameleon

Life-Changing Wisdom for Anyone Who Has a Personality or Knows Someone Who Does

Student Edition

The Chameleon

*Life-Changing Wisdom for Anyone Who Has a
Personality or Knows Someone Who Does*

Student Edition

By Merrick Rosenberg

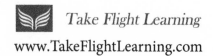

Take Flight Learning

www.TakeFlightLearning.com

Take Flight Learning
TakeFlightLearning.com
ChiefParrot@TakeFlightLearning.com

Copyright © 2018 by Take Flight Media

Second Edition 2017

ISBN-10: 0-9964110-0-3
ISBN-13: 978-0-9964110-0-4
eISBN-10: 0-9964110-2-X
eISBN-13: 978-0-9964110-2-8
Library of Congress Control Number: 2015957242

Dedication

To my parents, Barbara and Howard Rosenberg,
I am who I am because of you.
Thanks for believing.

To my wife, Traci, you fill my world with light.
Thank you for making my life an incredible adventure.

To my children, Gavin and Ben,
you make me smile every day.
Thanks for being you.

And if you are wondering if there are parts of this book
specifically about you . . . yes, there are.
Thanks for the inspiration.

Acknowledgments

I want thank all those who made this book possible. I am indebted to the support and insight you shared so willingly.

I am deeply grateful to be surrounded by such an amazing team of committed and hardworking individuals. To Jeff Backal, thanks for joining me on this journey—but get ready, because we've still got a long way to go.

To those who tirelessly introduce the birds to people all around the world, specifically, Andy Kraus, and Rick Kauffman, you lead the way in making a difference in so many lives.

To Dolores Woodington, Cathryn Plum, Elanna Grant, and Laura Williams, thank you for everything you do. This parrot would be lost without you.

To Kerry Bayles, Heather Hafner, and Valerie Vincent, it warms my heart to see the joy, laughter and transformation you bring to everyone you encounter on your travels.

I also want to thank all of those who provided feedback throughout the writing process, including Traci Rosenberg, Anouk Backal, Laura Robinson and Darah Backal.

To Matthew and Joan Greenblatt at CenterPointeMedia, thank you for your wisdom and focused attention to detail in bringing this book to life. I also want to thank Richard Ellis, Nesta Aharoni and Terrin Irwin for your gift of words and Michael Clarida and Nathan Davis for illustrating the characters into existence.

Finally, I want express my appreciation to all of the Certified Affiliates and Certified Trainers of Take Flight Learning. Your work sends ripples of positive energy and growth throughout the planet.

Contents

Spring

Summer

Fall

Winter

Foreword

I first encountered the DISC styles concept in 1974 while working on my PhD dissertation at Georgia State University. It was also the first time I taught it to a corporate group in Atlanta. I couldn't believe how the eyes of the audience lit up as they discovered the value and applicability of the four DISC styles. And here I am some 43+ years later with audiences still excited about the concept and what it means to their own self-enlightenment and improved interpersonal relationships. In 1974, I didn't know that I would travel more than 12 million miles worldwide and write more than 30 books to spread the word about DISC's universal wisdom.

The DISC styles have enriched my life immeasurably. I've learned how to treat others how *they* want to be treated, not how I want to be treated. Without DISC, I would have missed some of the best experiences of my life and hurt meaningful relationships. DISC has been a guide through the interpersonal moments that matter most.

When I met Merrick Rosenberg, I sensed a kindred spirit. We were both living the same mission on opposite sides of the country—me in California and Merrick in New Jersey, my old stomping ground where I graduated high school. I saw the same fire burning in him that was ignited in me all those years ago at Georgia State. It was clear that Merrick was living his life's purpose by sharing the DISC styles with the world.

Merrick's approach was fresh and different. Rather than using letters or descriptive words to identify the styles, he linked them to four birds. I could see how the visual nature of the eagles, parrots, doves and owls would make them much easier to remember and explain to others than just the four DISC letters.

But it wasn't just the birds that made Merrick's approach game-changing. Today, people want information mixed with entertainment, and Merrick grasped the power of teaching the styles through fables. He is a natural-born storyteller, and his fables go beyond mere explanation. He creates a landscape and immerses readers smack dab in the middle of the action.

In *The Chameleon*, Merrick skillfully depicts the challenges that stand in the way of happiness and success. The interactions between the birds are at once humorous and enlightening. In one fable, he deftly demonstrates how men and women perceive the DISC styles differently. In another, he shows what happens when opposites attract. Through it all, we learn to perceive the impact of our actions on others.

I am particularly excited about this second edition of *The Chameleon*. I appreciate how Merrick expanded on how to *Be the Chameleon* in one's daily life. Whether you are familiar with the DISC styles or encountering them for the first time, these fables and the accompanying chameleon wisdom will enrich your life. From your connection with your family to how you act in the workplace, *The Chameleon* can lead you to greater joy and well-being.

I hope you enjoy *The Chameleon* as much as I did, and may its learning reach deeply into your life.

Dr. Tony Alessandra, author of *The Platinum Rule*
and Hall-of-Fame Keynote Speaker

Preface

Prior to 1994 I thought I understood people. And why wouldn't I? I had earned an MBA specializing in organizational behavior. I had started one of the first team building companies in the United States, and it was thriving. Each day I taught people about teamwork, trust, communication, and leadership. Of course I understood people.

Then I discovered the DISC model, which described four personality styles that provided a framework for understanding behavior. Through this model I gained deep insight into my own needs, desires, motivators, and fears. I learned how to read people and proactively anticipate their needs. And the more I practiced applying these insights, the more I felt as if I had been living in the dark.

As I developed a new understanding of myself and others, a bright light began to shine on me and everyone else I knew. I never could have imagined something so simple could be so powerful.

For the next fifteen years, I traveled the world helping individuals increase their self-awareness and apply the wisdom of the styles. I watched people improve their relationships, increase their effectiveness at work, enhance their careers, and become better parents and partners. I was living my life's purpose. What more could I ask for?

Then I started to notice a pattern. While I felt gratified when attendees at my sessions shared how much they enjoyed my presentations, many of them added a question afterward that went something like this: "I think I'm a D. Which one is that again?" Or, "If I recall correctly, I'm an S. What does that stand for?"

I became deflated. How could this be? I was spending my days illuminating people's lives with the DISC styles, and the recipients weren't remembering the most basic lessons from those sessions. This revelation cast a shadow of doubt on the value of the training I was providing.

After one such encounter, I sat down to continue writing my new book about the DISC styles. I was excited to be halfway done, even though my enthusiasm had become tempered by an inner voice questioning the effectiveness of the four letters. That was the day I opened myself to the possibility that there must be a better way.

In a mere moment the idea of using four birds revealed itself to me. Perhaps my own parrot, Merlin, worked his magic by appearing in my mind's eye and enthusiastically symbolizing the Interactive I-style. "That's interesting," I thought. "I bet a parrot representing the I-style would be easier for people to remember."

Almost immediately an eagle confidently stepped forward to represent the perfect symbol of the Dominant D-style. Moments later, an owl logically showed himself to be the ideal Conscientious C. Next arrived a dove, who humbly offered to depict the Supportive S. And so it was. The birds were born.

I began introducing the birds into my training programs and speaking events, and I was astounded by the positive reception they received. In nearly every session, someone told me about their previous training and how they had forgotten everything afterwards. But the birds, they said, made the styles easier to remember and apply. During fifteen years as a trainer and speaker, I had been using four letters that provided only a fleeting fascination. The birds, however, were creating lasting change.

As an increasing number of people began sharing stories of the birds' impact, I could not help but wonder what made them so special. At first, I chalked it up to our common impression of each bird's nature, which made them memorable. An owl, for example, instantly conjures up images of logic and precision, making the C-style easy to recall.

But it was more than that. Soon I recognized that people's memory challenges had been rooted in the letters themselves. When the words "Dominant," "Interactive," "Supportive," and "Conscientious" were shortened to D, I, S, and C, they were stripped of their meaning, which made them harder to remember. Unlike the image of an eagle, the letter D meant nothing and, therefore, had no sticking power. The D-I-S-C letters, quite simply, were not brain-friendly.

Applying new insights requires remembering those insights. The birds provide mental models that do just that. In contrast to the DISC acronym, the birds are mnemonic devices or memory aids. Just like "Every Good Boy Does Fine" helps budding musicians remember the lines of the treble clef, the four birds help people remember the four personality styles.

Now, when I meet people long after they have attended a session that incorporated the bird styles, I regularly hear statements such as, "I am a dove" or "I am a parrot with a little bit of eagle." Those pronouncements are often followed by stories about how the styles are playing out in their lives.

When the birds flew into my world, the trajectory of my life changed. I shelved the book in progress about the four letter styles and, instead, coauthored *Taking Flight*! with Daniel Silvert. In that book, the first to include the birds, we taught people about the styles and how to use them in daily interactions . . . and how to remember them!

In *The Chameleon*, I take that knowledge and application to the next level. While the characters in the book are birds and chameleons, the content is about you and everyone you know. Does the owl represent your boss? The dove your spouse or parent? Perhaps the parrot is a coworker and the eagle one of your children.

Before we begin this journey, let's review some foundational principles of style. To begin with, each one of us is a combination of all four styles. Nobody is just an eagle, parrot, dove, or owl. We all have a bit of each style within us, and, if we incorporate some flexibility, we can display any of the behaviors . . . despite our natural style.

There are no good or bad styles. Each has its own strengths and challenges. And two people who share the same style may display that style to varying degrees.

One person may be a pygmy owl, displaying slight tendencies of the owl style. Another may be the great horned owl, strongly exemplifying owl behaviors in just about everything they do.

We all get caught up in the drama of our life stories, just as the birds get caught up in theirs. Take a page out of this book and become the chameleon. Flexibly adapt to the people you encounter and the situations that unfold around you. As you read each fable, mindfully look inside yourself and consider how the lessons presented apply in your life.

It's time to tap into the wisdom of *The Chameleon*!

Introduction

The Journey Begins

A s the sun rose over the Great Lake, Xenia gazed at the dawn of a new era. She adjusted her chameleon skin to match the crimson dawn and then harmonized her coloring with the morning sky as it migrated from orange, gold, and yellow and to soothing daylight blue.

Chameleons have an innate wisdom that allows them to connect to the world and to those around them. Xenia was no exception. She instinctively understood how to handle life's situations with grace and ease. Her intuition, coupled with insight passed down by her father, enabled her to ask the right question at the right moment, and to inspire profound transformation.

Xenia considered herself fortunate to be the daughter of Xavier, a wise and generous master chameleon. She had spent many days shadowing him in the forest, believing he knew nothing of her presence. In retrospect, she now understood that he knew everything of her presence. From a young age, Xavier had taught her to live her life lessons responsibly and to share them with others. Clearly, it was Xenia's duty to pass on her wisdom to the next generation of chameleons as well as to all of the other animals dwelling in the forest she called Home.

Today, Xenia was taking her newest chameleon student, Xander, on his first walk through Home. In time, she would introduce him to the forest's many residents and teach him to sing the song of the birds. She would open his heart to what she had learned when she was young and inexperienced. One day, her student would travel throughout the land and share his lessons—and so the cycle would continue.

Despite her student's young age, Xenia would not treat him as a child. Instead, she would offer him respect and speak to him as if she were awakening a deep knowledge that was sleeping inside him.

Xander arrived early, eager to begin the day, and Xenia did not waste any time. She began, "Everything in life is connected. When one element of the world falls out of balance, waves of discontent ripple throughout the land. I will teach you to anticipate and navigate those ripples. You will learn to appear at the moment you are needed and to nudge life back into balance. You will experience oneness with the forest and all who live here. One day, you will teach those who come after you."

Xenia smiled as she recognized that her words resonated deeply with her student. In his short life, Xander had seen great unease circulate among the creatures of Home, and he wanted to play his part in drawing the forest residents together again.

The teacher continued. "For a while, you will travel with me and observe what I do and how I do it. You will remain unseen at all times and will not reveal yourself unless I announce your presence. Even then, you will remain silent unless a question is directly asked of you. Understood?"

"Understood," the young chameleon affirmed.

"It's time to expand your world in every way," Xenia proclaimed. "To begin, here's a map of the forest. In order to help others find their way, you must first be able to find your own."

Xander reached out to take the map and nodded gratefully.

"Today we will practice the art of invisibility," Xenia said.

"I'm ready," replied Xander with a twinge of excitement. He was elated that a living legend had taken him under her wing.

The pair walked in silence, shifting their coloring to match the varying terrain that evolved beneath them. They walked past bashful blossoms, bulky boulders, and towering pines.

After smoothly crossing a gentle stream, they came upon a family of white doves. Xenia placed a single finger over her mouth, indicating to Xander that they were to stop and observe in silence. The chameleons watched the considerate doves prepare their morning meal and share their bounty with friends. They listened to interested doves ask each other questions about the upcoming day. They noticed supportive doves help a companion who was dealing with a challenging situation. The birds' warm tones and gentle demeanors prompted Xander to smile.

After a few minutes of observation, Xenia advanced Xander onward. "What did you feel emanating from the doves?" Xenia asked her new student.

Xander replied, "Kindness and gentleness. I liked the way they listened to each other. They genuinely care about everyone else's feelings and about the events occurring in each others' lives."

"Very perceptive," replied the teacher. "What do you draw from that?"

Xander glanced once more at the doves and added, "That they are supportive and cooperative, and that they are calm."

"Right again, young sir," Xenia confirmed. "Doves are generally soft spoken and patient. They embody harmony and compassion."

As the chameleons continued on, they transformed from the emerald-olive shades of the vibrant ground cover to the earthy, rich tones of the unassuming stones and twigs. They continued to walk until Xenia spotted a pair of owls nestled in a maple tree. They were planning their day's activities. The observers settled in silence a short distance away.

"We can't get too close to the owls," Xenia advised. "Everything about them is sharp and accurate, including their powers of observation. If we get too close, they will notice us and change their behavior. Let's watch from here."

The owls were busy organizing their belongings and returning various items to their designated places. While one of the owls talked about a problem he was having, the other asked him question after question. The detailed answers and discussions that followed led both owls to explore a series of alternative solutions and then choose a course of action.

After a few minutes, Xenia asked her protégé, "What can you draw from the owls' behavior?"

"They are very structured," Xander said. "They were operating from a checklist while they were organizing their belongings. I'll bet even their checklists have checklists!"

"Perhaps they do," Xenia chuckled.

The chameleons continued to watch quietly as the owls created a plan for the day.

Xander added, "They are very careful and precise."

"Quite accurate, my little friend," Xenia confirmed. "They are analytical by nature and enjoy working through complex problems."

The teacher and student continued onward. They traveled over gently sloping hills and hiked passed the mountainous Xanadu's Peak. Xenia gave a slight bow to the impressive peak, which had been named after the wise chameleon master, Xanadu.

"What was so great about Xanadu?" Xander wondered aloud.

Xenia's bright, yellow eyes grew wider still. "When I was your age, my father, Xavier, taught me Xanadu's guiding principle of the forest: Treat others how they need to be treated. We now call it the Home Rule."

Xander looked puzzled, but he didn't want to challenge his teacher. Xenia noticed his expression and prompted him to speak his mind.

Xander offered, "Well, it's just that my parents taught me that I am supposed to treat others how *I* want to be treated."

"Ah! That is one of the great truths of all forests throughout the land."

"I'm confused. What you just said is opposite of what my parents taught me. Which one is right? Treat others how *I* want to be treated or how *they* want to be treated?"

Xenia laughed. "Sometimes the opposite of great wisdom is more great wisdom. When it comes to virtues such as kindness, respect, and fairness, you should treat others how *you* want to be treated. When you do that, those virtues will be returned to you in abundance. But when you share information, provide instructions, or offer praise, you should treat others how *they* want to be treated. You see, both statements are true."

Xander still looked puzzled as Xenia continued. "In our walks together, keep your eyes open and notice how often the birds impose their style of doing things on others. In the meantime, I hear the parrots up ahead. Let's listen in."

The chameleons did not need to get too close to hear a group of parrots who were telling stories. At times, several stories were circulating at once. When one parrot started a story, another jumped in with her own. Moments later the first parrot continued. None of them seemed to mind the interruptions.

"They sure like to talk!" Xander noted. "And they sound fun."

"Oh, they are," Xenia replied. "What else do you notice?"

Xander laughed. "They seem excited about something. They are bursting with energy!"

"They are not just excited about what they are talking about. They live in a perpetual state of optimism and enthusiasm. Parrots are easy to observe. It's a good thing we can find them everywhere."

"Great! Who's next?" Xander exclaimed, speaking as if he had caught some parrot spirit.

"Look up," the chameleon directed.

They moved to a clearing so they could view the sky above the treetops. Just below the clouds, Xander spotted a lone eagle floating on a current. Her expression was focused and intense. Clearly, she was not flying for the fun of it. She was working. The eagle glided effortlessly until, suddenly, she snapped her head to the right. Without hesitation, she rocketed towards the lake like a meteorite.

"Wow!" Xander exclaimed. "She seems to be on a mission!"

Just then the eagle emerged with a large fish and began to soar to the clouds.

"Once she knows what she wants, there is no stopping her," Xenia replied. "What else did you see?"

"Well, before she dove, she was studying the entire forest."

"Very perceptive," Xenia affirmed. "When you want to watch an eagle, look to the sky. They view the world from a vantage point above the daily details of life. Eagles are direct, decisive, and focused on bottom-line results."

Before the chameleons started their return home, they climbed to the top of the nearest tree and stood on its highest branch. Xenia smiled at her new student and said, "Today you met the four major birds of the forest and learned an important lesson: treat others how *they* need to be treated. Together we will observe the birds and, occasionally, intervene to guide them to greater understanding. By helping them, you will learn the ways of the chameleon. Are you ready to join me on this path of discovery?"

"Absolutely," affirmed her student.

Xenia looked out across the treetops and said, "So it begins. Let us journey together and learn how to take flight."

Spring

The New Addition

The forest, affectionately known as Home, echoed with the sights and sounds of the cheerful promise of spring. Trees began to reveal traces of a woodland green that had been hibernating all winter. New life sprouted in all directions. A budding kaleidoscope of floral colors signaled a transition was on the way.

The birds were already awake as the forest was emerging from its long winter slumber. Settled high in the swaying trees, they sang excitedly—especially the parrots, whose laughter echoed throughout the land. The eagles soared mightily among fluffy clouds that bid "good morning" to all. The owls were barely visible. Their bark-like feathers obscured them from view, which enabled them to keep a watchful eye on the myriad forms of life that scurried below them.

Walking through Home on this fresh spring morning, the chameleons followed the path of a meandering stream. After passing a grove of wise, old elm trees, they came across a single mighty oak. With his eyes, Xander followed its trunk to its highest point. Thinking he saw something at the top, he squinted, trying to zoom in on the image.

The young chameleon pointed and asked, "Is that an eagle up there?"

"It sure is," Xenia smiled. "That's Sadie. She and her parents have been old friends of mine for a long time. I've known her since the day she first appeared in her parents' lives."

"She looks strong and confident," Xander proclaimed. "I'll bet she was pretty headstrong when she was young."

"Oh, you don't know the half of it," said Xenia. "The day I first met her was a day just like today. My father and I watched from a distance as Samuel and Sarah shook their white dove feathers as if they were releasing the cold winter from their bones. They awoke to the soft cooing sounds of their new little doves, whose tiny white feathers poked outward like miniature stems waiting to bloom."

"As the sun reached the edge of the horizon, the youngsters opened their eyes to the light of the new day. Though they were hungry, they didn't complain. They instinctively knew food was on its way. Sarah stood guard over her brood as Samuel searched for provisions for his expanding family."

"Just as he collected his first catch of the day, Samuel heard a high-pitched squeal from beyond a small stand of trees. He approached cautiously. He peeked behind a mighty oak and was astonished. A baby eagle was staring back at him. The dove looked around for the eagle's parents, but no one was in sight. Samuel yelled out to the forest, but nobody answered."

"Did the parents come to get her?" Xander asked.

"They did not," Xenia answered.

"So what did you do?"

"I watched," Xenia smirked. "Chameleons do not manipulate situations; we adapt to what is. We make small suggestions that can create big impacts. We gently help others see the path that is for the greatest good of everyone involved."

Xenia continued her story. "Samuel shouted to the treetops, 'There's a baby eagle down here! Don't worry, she's all right!' But still no answer. He searched the skies but did not see any adult eagles. He waited and waited, but nobody came for the baby. He couldn't leave the helpless little one alone, so he did what came naturally to him. He scooped up the baby bird and placed her safely under his wing."

"When Samuel returned home, Sarah was upset with him. As Samuel approached her, she called out, 'I've been so worried. What took you so long?' Before Samuel could answer, Sarah noticed the scrawny eagle. Immediately, her heart melted and she wanted to help. As she began to comfort the young one, she directed nearby doves to find food and create a safe shelter for the baby."

"Days later, after an alert had been dispatched throughout Home, the baby eagle's parents still had not been found. The doves searched the forest and talked to everyone they knew, but nobody came forward to claim her. Samuel and Sarah cared for the eagle, and, day by day, grew to love her. They accepted the eagle as their own. They named her Sadie."

"Did you or your father do anything to help the doves?" Xander wondered.

"We did not," Xenia replied. "But I recall my father warning them about turbulent times ahead. Over the years, Sadie grew strong and confident. Soon she grew larger than her adoptive parents. Yet despite her size, she had much to learn. Samuel and Sarah spent a great deal of time teaching Sadie the ways of the doves. As they did with their own children, they conveyed the values and behaviors of contributing members in a community. They taught her how to be kind and thoughtful. They discussed the importance of listening with compassion and putting the needs of others ahead of oneself."

"The eagle gained much from her parents. She learned to speak kindly, although occasionally she offended her dove siblings with her frankness. She loved to play games, but often had to be reminded to be gracious if she lost. Sadie hated losing. She preferred to do things on her own, which Sarah lovingly described as Sadie's 'little independent streak.'"

"As Sadie grew older, she began to feel as if she didn't fit in with her family. When she reached the age nestled between childhood and adulthood, she confided to her dove siblings that she was uncomfortable with many of their ways. Their ways didn't feel natural to her. Her brothers and sisters didn't know how to remedy her unease so they simply offered words of comfort and a promise to always be there for her. Sadie smiled at them and held her tongue, as she had been taught to do."

"A few weeks ago Sadie befriended a fellow eagle. She has been enjoying his company and adopting some of his eagle ways. Lately, Sadie has been confidently speaking her mind and decisively taking charge when things needed to get done. She is losing some of the listening skills that her parents painstakingly instilled in her, but she is gaining other eagle skills."

"Do her parents notice the changes?" Xander asked.

"They do. Sarah and Samuel attribute the changes to her age. However, others in the dove community are dropping hints about what they call 'Sadie's directness,' and I believe they are preparing to talk with her about it."

The chameleons continued walking and enjoying the bright spring morning. Throughout the following week, they observed the dove's large eagle youngster disregarding the values her adoptive parents had instilled in her. At one point, the chameleons overheard Samuel and Sarah debating whether they should talk with Sadie about it. While the two dove parents did not like confrontation, they felt it was important to intervene before their eagle's 'little independent streak' offended someone.

For days, the dove parents agonized over how to best approach Sadie about this growing problem. They didn't want to offend her. The doves decided to prepare a nice meal, then dismiss their other children so they could talk to Sadie over her favorite dessert. Slowly, Samuel and Sarah edged their way into the discussion. Sadie had almost completely finished her treat before they finally got to the point.

The chameleon pair listened as Sarah began. "Sadie, there's something your dad and I want to speak with you about. Is that all right?"

"Okay," shrugged the eagle.

"Your father and I have noticed that since you have been spending time with other eagles, you have been . . ." she paused to collect her thoughts. "What I'm trying to say is that when you speak . . . how should I say this?"

She looked to Samuel for assistance. "What your mother is trying to say is that lately you haven't been as nice as usual when you are speaking to others. Is something wrong? Is anything bothering you?"

"Nope. I'm good," replied the eagle.

"Have you noticed how you have been speaking to others recently?" Sarah asked. "It's not as gentle as we taught you."

"I feel great. In fact, I've never felt better."

The doves were unsure about where to go next. Then the eagle added, "I've always had a hard time *softening my words*. Now, I feel like I'm just being me."

Samuel and Sarah didn't know how to respond.

"You don't have to worry about me. I'm fine," concluded the eagle.

With that, Sadie rose to clean up her food. She assumed the conversation was over. Before the doves could say anything more, Sadie leapt from the dove family tree and flew off to spend time with her new friends. The frustrated parents shook their heads as Sarah concluded, "Well, that didn't go as well as I had hoped."

"Is it time to help them out?" Xander squirmed.

"Indeed," replied Xenia.

As the sun's light began to fade and brilliant stars materialized overhead, the parents discussed their dilemma. They had never faced anything like this with their other children, and they did not know what do.

From a nearby branch, Xenia instructed her young apprentice to remain in the shadows. She was going to transform into the color of a bright green leaf that sat beside the dove pair. Suddenly, Xenia burst into the conversation, "Good evening, my friends."

Sarah smiled. "Welcome. It is so nice to see you, Xenia."

The chameleon gave a slight bow of her head and with a gentle smile expressed, "My father sends his regards."

The three old friends spoke at length about the eagle. The chameleon listened with empathy and compassion, just as the doves would have for anyone who shared their problems with them.

When the doves were finished expressing their dilemma, Xenia reminded them of a previous conversation. "I remember the day my father and I were passing by your home. You had just accepted the young eagle into your family and had agreed to become her adoptive parents."

"I remember that discussion," Samuel recalled. He reflected on Xavier's prophetic words: "You will parent with love. You will treat your new addition the only way that you know how, and you will be wonderful parents. But there will come a day when Sadie will appear to change. You will feel as though she has become someone else. She may even become unrecognizable to you. When that day comes, realize that she has not become someone new, but rather, is developing into who she was born to be."

"That didn't make sense to me at the time," Samuel reflected.

"But now I understand," Sarah acknowledged.

"Sometimes it's not that we change," said the chameleon. "It's that we become who we truly are."

Samuel nodded. "I guess we have been trying to turn Sadie into someone she is not. We have been trying to turn her into a dove."

"Oh," Sarah sighed. "I hope we have not been sending a message that we do not accept her for who she is."

Xenia smiled. "As my father predicted, you have been wonderful parents. Now it is time to let her be who she was born to be."

Samuel and Sarah understood.

Xenia concluded, "Just as my father watched over you and your friends, I will watch over Sadie and hers."

Sarah was about to thank Xenia and tell her how much they appreciated her instinctive ability to adapt to any situation. Before Sarah could tell her chameleon friend that she could see her father's wisdom radiating from her clear eyes, Xenia was gone.

The next morning, Sadie rose with the first light of day. Samuel and Sarah, already awake, joined their daughter for a light breakfast. "Sadie," Samuel said, "we want you to know that we love you for who you are."

"We realize that we have been expecting you to act like a dove, but that is not your true nature," Sarah added.

Sadie smiled, "I appreciate the dove ways, but it's time for me to spread my wings and be an eagle."

They all looked up and saw her new eagle friend standing a few branches above them on an adjacent tree. "Hey, Dee," he called, using the nickname her new friends had given her. "You ready to go?"

The eagle pumped her large wings as she turned back to her parents and said, "You're the best. Thanks!"

Sarah grinned and said, "I guess her little independent streak isn't just a phase."

"I suppose it's not," Samuel agreed. "I suppose it's not."

Chameleon Wisdom

*Success means having the courage,
the determination, and the
will to become the person you
believe you were meant to be.*
—George Sheehan

The first step to happiness and success is living an authentic life—being yourself. Sometimes we suppress who we are because our natural style is not acceptable to others. The time period we live in creates cultural norms. Our parents tell us how we are supposed to act in social situations. The workplace defines a set of behavioral expectations based on organizational culture. The world around us constantly places pressure on us to fit in.

In *The New Addition*, Sadie (or Dee, as her friends call her) was taught by her parents how she should interact in the world, and she adapted her behavior to harmonize with her adopted dove family. But her eagle nature called to her to act differently. As Sadie struggled to adjust to the dove world, she sacrificed her true self. The resulting inner turmoil left her feeling never quite like herself. In the end, she stepped into her power and became the eagle she was meant to be. In doing so, she did not change her personality. Instead, she embraced it.

If who we are varies from the cultural norm, we often mask our preferences in order to gain approval. We put on social or career facades in our drive to be accepted.

Imagine an individual with a strong parrot nature—energetic, fun, optimistic—who works in a restrictive and restrained work environment. His manager is beginning to lose patience with his frequent interactions with coworkers. In order to maintain his employment, the parrot learns to bury his head in his computer and remain at his desk. He keeps conversations to a minimum and speaks quietly, making certain to minimize his enthusiasm about ideas and experiences. Due to a lack of human interaction, the parrot leaves work feeling more discontented each day. But he wants to keep his job, so he adjusts his behavior.

Eventually, the parrot becomes so dissatisfied at work that he leaves the company to find employment in an organization that allows him to embrace his authentic self. It doesn't take long for him to feel like himself again. A few months later, a former coworker joins his team and can't believe how much he has changed in such a short period time. In reality, he hasn't changed at all. The new environment has simply allowed him to remove his mask and be himself.

We cannot achieve our greatest potential and cultivate deep connections with others unless we live authentically. Acting like someone we are not drains us of valuable energy. Behaving in a way that conflicts with our style creates cognitive dissonance. When we really want to act *this* way, but feel as if we should act *that* way, our thoughts become incongruent. This leads to stress, frustration, anger, and even depression.

Reclaim who you were meant to be. Look inside yourself and identify who you are when you are living mask-free. Recognize when you are out of alignment with your true self, and dare to liberate your true nature. Value your innate gifts, and don't let others define you. Let go of the need for approval, and surround yourself with people who value you for who you are, not who they want you to be. Make a deep personal commitment to be yourself.

Throughout this book, you will discover how to tap into the wisdom of the chameleon. Understand, though, that there's a big difference between flexibly adapting to a temporary situation and changing who you are in order to adapt to a permanent one. Although adaptability takes place in the moment, you need not change who you are and what makes you special. Be honest with yourself, and allow your style to shine through.

The Chameleon Student

When we were young, the voice of our parents became an internal compass. They encouraged us to be honest and work hard. They chastised us when we were disrespectful and advised us to be kind. When our parents told us not to cheat, lie or steal, they tried to instill values that would last throughout our lifetimes. Today, their words still guide our behavior.

But, some of their advice emanated from their personality style rather than from an objective sense of right and wrong. Picture a Parrot mom suggesting that her daughter ought to make more friends, when, in fact, the young girl is happy having one best friend. Imagine an Owl dad telling his child to be more organized.

In those formative years, we internalized our parents' advice and directives. Their words became the greatest hits of our childhood, like songs played on repeat. Our parents probably repeated these old and tired lines because we never seemed to 'get' it. The behaviors they asked us to adopt may have run counter to our personality. If what they asked us to do was natural and within our style, we already would be doing it!

Our teenage years provided each of us with an opportunity to find our own voice – one that is grounded in our innate personality and bolstered by the values our parents worked tirelessly to impart.

As you transition into a new school and a new phase of life, consider whether you are living from your personality style or from someone else's expectations. Now is the perfect time to reinvent yourself if you want to. Don't become someone who you were told you were supposed to be. Instead, become who you truly are. Join clubs that accentuate your strengths. Participate in activities that will develop your latent desires. Let go of old activities that your parents signed you up for with the best of intentions. If you give your personality permission to shine in everything you do, you will find joy and success throughout your life.

- **GET TO KNOW YOURSELF.** Reflect on what you are doing when you are at your happiest.

- **STEP OUT OF YOUR COMFORT ZONE** and do what comes naturally.

- **PUT YOUR OWN NEEDS FIRST** instead of always aiming to please others. You are not good for others if you're not good to yourself.

- **DO NOT WORRY** about how others see you. Some people may not like who you truly are, but by being your authentic self, you will draw people into your life who do.

The Sparrow's Nest

The velvety, spring breeze contrasted with the rough, destructive storm that had just passed through the forest. Powerful winds had snapped even the strongest branches, dislodging and destroying many nests. No one had been seriously injured, but the sparrows suffered the greatest loss at the worst time for them. Just as they were about to grow their families, they found themselves homeless.

Fortunately, the sparrows were prepared for such an event. They had stockpiled hundreds of Sparrow Nest Kits, which now could be assembled quickly.

Volunteers came from the four corners of Home to support the nest rebuilding efforts. Helpers were organized in groups of two, and each partnership was tasked with building five nests. After signing in, Carl and Ivory joined forces to assemble their kits.

As an owl, Carl was analytical and renowned for doing things right the first time. He liked to think before acting and had a knack for staying organized. He specialized in accuracy and quality, traits that would serve his nest-building partnership well.

As a parrot, Ivory was brimming with positive energy. She understood how difficult this time was for the sparrows, so she focused on helping rebuild homes that were even better and stronger than before. Her contagious passion and enthusiasm would help her partner stay motivated and upbeat while completing their project.

The owl and the parrot set out to find the perfect tree in which to place their first nest. Ivory excitedly pointed out several locations, but none of them met Carl's precise standards. Eventually, an ideal spot was identified, and the pair felt ready to begin construction. As they laid the nest kits on the ground near the tree, Carl reassured his parrot friend, "Do not worry, Ivory. I will keep us on track."

Ivory wasn't sure what Carl meant by that, but because she was so eager to begin, she let his comment go. Immediately, the parrot started energetically pulling materials out of the first kit. At the same time, Carl was carefully inspecting each item to make sure nothing had been damaged. He inspected the stems, roots, and leaves for cracks. He scrutinized the grass, feathers, string, and papers and compared them with the diagrams decorating the instructions.

Knowing they had five nests to build, Ivory was itching to begin. She made comments such as "These nests aren't going to build themselves," but her commentary did not speed Carl up a bit. So . . . she waited while the owl focused his attention on the details, tapping her toe impatiently all the while.

Once Carl was certain all parts were in suitable condition, he meticulously lined up the materials and sorted them into precise piles according to their components.

"We are almost ready to begin," Carl announced. "All the parts are in acceptable condition. Now we have to count the pieces to make sure we have the right number of each item."

Ivory gasped. "What do you mean? We just opened a brand new kit. I'm sure it's all here."

"You cannot trust that the kit is right. It is best to count the items and be certain. You may wish to remember this the next time you have to assemble something."

Ivory shook her head incredulously as she watched Carl match the supplies to the checklist. If she had been working alone, she would have had this first nest assembled already. She couldn't imagine having to endure the owl's tedious process four more times!

After confirming that the inventory was accurate, Carl suggested, "Let's read through the instructions before we begin. We do not want any surprises. Would you like to read the directions aloud?"

"Read through the instructions?" the parrot exclaimed. "Are you serious? I think it's pretty obvious how these parts come together. I've seen many sparrow nests. Haven't you?"

Carl was getting frustrated with Ivory's impatience. "Of course I have seen sparrows' nests, but seeing one is not the same as building one. We do not want the nest to fall apart in a storm. There is a right way and a wrong way to assemble a nest. I prefer the right way. Don't you?"

Ivory took a consoling deep breath. She didn't want to spend the day arguing with Carl, so she made a suggestion: "How about this? Let's start assembling the nests, and if we need the instructions, we can refer to them. I've watched many sparrows build nests, and it's always looked pretty easy."

"I am sure it did not *look* difficult, but that is because the sparrows knew what they were doing. You saw sparrows building sparrows' nests, after all. I have watched owls build many things throughout my life. But being an owl does not mean I can create what I observed without careful planning. One day you may be able to apply this particular process to future projects, and you might even discover that being organized serves you well."

Ivory inhaled deeply. In the interest of collaboration, she accepted Carl's terms. Step by step, piece by piece, the sparrow's nest painstakingly took form. At one point Ivory tried to infuse some positive energy into the meticulous process by announcing, "This is looking good. I'm feeling more like a sparrow every minute!"

Carl immediately replied, "This is more complicated than it seems. Let us not develop a false sense of security. We can celebrate when we are finished."

Ivory rolled her eyes, but Carl was too busy securing a twig into the structure to notice. The parrot continued to read through the steps in the instructions . . . one by one . . . as she watched her owl partner faultlessly add each element to the nest. After placing a piece, he tested the nest for structural integrity. Each part passed his test, without fail.

After finishing the outer layer of the nest, Carl declared, "We have now completed half the steps. So far this nest is solid."

"Sure is," Ivory replied halfheartedly.

"Before this day is over, you will have developed the building skills of an owl," Carl joked. "What, Ivory, no enthusiastic pronouncements that this is the best nest you have ever seen? No exclamations about how awesome we are for making something so incredible? Where is your parrot spirit?"

Ivory deadpanned, "Yeah. It's great. Very proud."

But Ivory wasn't happy or proud. In fact, she was becoming increasingly upset. The owl's words felt like a personal attack. Ivory reflected on other things she had assembled in her life. She had always seemed to figure it out. She was frustrated that Carl did not trust her to play a more important role than merely reading the instructions. And his snail's pace was maddening to her.

Ivory remained silent during the building of the first nest, but after that she couldn't take it anymore. Before opening the second kit, she decided it was time to speed things up. "How about you read the instructions to me this time?" Ivory requested.

Carl felt less than confident in the role of reader, but he felt compelled to agree. "Uh, sure," he answered.

"Great. What's first?"

Before Carl could even pick up the instructions, Ivory pointed to a nearby tree and declared, "That's the one. We'll put it right there."

The parrot ripped open the second kit, pulled out the directions, tossed them aside, and started to build. As Carl watched her weave seemingly random items together, he recalled the process that he had just followed. He had a bad feeling about this second nest.

Ivory noticed Carl's worried look as she inserted a long twig into the bottom section. She smiled reassuringly and said, "Don't worry, Carl. Sometimes letting go of instructions and following your gut is the best way to work."

Carl didn't know what to say. He could see that Ivory was not going to follow the instructions, so he put them down and helped her as much as he could. Occasionally, he made subtle suggestions, such as "Wouldn't it be best if we put this piece in before that one?"

Carl was open to her ideas, but from his analytical perspective, her way was not the way to assemble a nest . . . or anything else, for that matter.

Every now and then, Ivory asked Carl to retrieve a part or questioned him about a specific piece. By the time Carl provided all the information she asked for, Ivory was two steps ahead of him. At one point Ivory commented cheerfully, "You see, Carl, sometimes in life you have to forget the rules and just make things happen. Life is meant to be enjoyed, not organized. You need to live more in the moment and not worry so much about the details."

They completed the second nest in half the time it took to build the first. Sure, they had a few parts left over, and Ivory had to redo some pieces and go back a few steps with others, but "that's how it goes when you're building something," enthused Ivory.

The parrot took a step back to marvel at their creation. She concluded, "This is not bad for two non-sparrows."

Carl nodded without saying a word. "What's wrong?" Ivory probed. "You should be proud of this nest. Look at the quality craftsmanship," she beamed.

"I think we each define 'quality craftsmanship' differently," said Carl. "But what bothers me most is how you treated me while we were building the second nest."

"What do you mean?" Ivory wondered. "We built the nest quickly, and it looks pretty darn good."

"Yes, it is complete, but I would have gone about it differently," Carl explained. "Did you notice how smoothly the first nest went? I respected the process and you played a vital role."

"A vital role?" puzzled the parrot. "I did nothing and the process took forever. That's not how I like to work."

"Are you saying you did not appreciate the focus and methodology we employed in building the first nest?"

"I did not appreciate it, and you made me feel incompetent and unimportant," Ivory explained. "All I did was read the instructions to you."

"I felt similarly while we were building the second nest," Carl acknowledged. "You made me feel like my approach to the project was wrong."

"Seriously?"

"Seriously."

"This conversation reminds me of something that Xenia once taught me," Ivory recalled.

"What's that?" asked the owl.

"Well, one day, I was talking with Simon, who is such a helpful dove. He had just agreed to assist our favorite eagle, Dee, with a river cleanup project, even though he had no time to do it. But you know Simon. He likes to be supportive, and he didn't want to say no."

"I understand that," said Carl.

"I approached Simon after Dee left, and I told him he needs to be more assertive. I explained that there are times we have to stand up for ourselves and that he doesn't always have to put the needs of others ahead of his own. At that moment, Xenia appeared."

"She has a way of doing that," the owl observed.

"Tell me about it!" laughed the parrot. "That chameleon always pops up at just the right moment. Anyway, Xenia said that . . ."

All of sudden, a cheery voiced inserted itself into their conversation. "Did I hear my name?"

Carl and Ivory nearly fell off of their branch.

"Your timing is impeccable!" Ivory announced. "Can you shed some light on what we're discussing? I'm guessing you heard the whole thing."

Xenia smiled and replied, "I would be glad to."

Carl grabbed a piece of paper so he could capture her wisdom.

"You're going to write Xenia's words down?" Ivory asked.

"Yes, I am," Carl grinned. "Does that bother you?"

"Nope. Not at all," Ivory giggled.

Xenia waited until Carl was ready and then shared. "When you try to change someone's personality, you send a message to them that the way they are is not okay."

Just then a squirrel scurried by holding several nuts she had just unburied. The threesome watched as she zigged and zagged her way through the forest, seemingly unsure of where to go next. As Carl and Ivory stared in amusement, Carl considered the implications of Xenia's words. He rolled up the paper and tucked the scroll away for safekeeping. "I understand," Carl said. "That is what I did to Ivory. I was not just telling her to follow the instructions, I was also expecting her to act like an owl."

"Precisely," Xenia confirmed.

"What I heard from my owl friend was that it was not okay for me to be a parrot," Ivory shared. "Carl was trying to change me into an owl—to not accept me for who I am."

"I never thought about it like that," Carl acknowledged.

"I know that wasn't your intention, but that's how I felt."

"I apologize for my actions," added Carl. "I suppose that is how I felt, too. When you asked me not to follow a process I am accustomed to, I felt as if you were not only discounting my abilities, but also not letting me be an owl. It felt like you were saying that being a parrot is better than being an owl."

"I see that now," Ivory confirmed. "I'm sorry about that."

"How about this," Carl suggested. "We have three more nests to build. Let's put the instructions aside and start working on the next one. What do you think?"

"Can you do that?" Ivory wondered.

"Not sure," Carl admitted. "But I am willing to give it a try."

"Does this mean we're not going to take an inventory of the parts?" Ivory asked with a teasing glint in her eye.

"Let's not get too crazy," Carl replied. "Sparrows need to live in these nests."

"That sounds like a good compromise. How about we just accept that you are an owl and I am a parrot? Together we will find a way to build that works for both of us."

"Sounds like a plan," Carl replied. "Can I hold the instructions for safekeeping?"

Ivory agreed cheerfully.

The pair turned around to thank Xenia for her help. "Hey, where'd she go?" Ivory asked.

"She is gone. She seems to do that a lot," Carl smiled.

The parrot and the owl spent the next few hours constructing the remaining three nests. They worked well together and compromised as they sought to understand one another's style. When they were done with their building project, they were both proud of what they had accomplished . . . together.

Chameleon Wisdom

Never try to teach a pig to sing.
It wastes your time and it
annoys the pig.
—Robert Heinlein

Think about someone close to you who has a habit you have tried to change. Perhaps this person is your partner, child, or coworker. How much energy have you applied to trying to change this individual's behavior? Did your effort make a difference? If they did make the change, did the change stick, or did they eventually revert back to their old ways, leaving you even more frustrated than before?

Now consider the emotional impact on you and on the person you tried to change. What effect did your efforts have on you, and what underlying message were you sending to the other person?

In *The Sparrow's Nest*, Carl and Ivory imposed their styles on each other. By insisting on following their own methodology for building nests, they unwittingly devalued the approach of the other. This ultimately led to frustration and conflict.

Imagine a family in which a father with an intense eagle style is constantly telling his humble and soft-spoken dove child to act more assertively. Picture that parent at a soccer game yelling from the sidelines, "Stop smiling and focus! Attack the ball! Don't wait for him to come to you!"

The eagle father thinks he is helping his child improve his skills and get better results. However, the message received by the dove child is, "I am bad at soccer, and I am not the person my father wants me to be."

The child who was previously enjoying a soccer game with his friends now feels badly about himself and no longer wants to play. In addition, his self-esteem has taken a hit.

When you judge the way others act, you send the message that who they are is not okay. In contrast, when you accept someone fully, you validate that person's worth. Accepting others for who they are, rather than for who you want them to be, replaces judgment with acceptance. This acceptance creates the foundation for a meaningful connection.

However, acceptance of others does not preclude the importance of giving constructive feedback. In fact, it is the role of a parent or a manager to help those under their wings to learn, grow, and prosper. Balance constructive feedback with positive reinforcement that highlights strengths.

Finally, there's a big difference between addressing a single action and addressing a pattern of behavior that is rooted in someone's personality. When you try to change an overarching behavioral trait, recognize that you are not just asking that person to adjust what they do, you are also asking them to change their core nature. Be careful and compassionate.

The Chameleon Student

As the birds learned in *The Sparrows Nest,* when we try to change others, we send the inadvertent message that who they are is not okay. Teachers are not immune to this mistake. Go back in time to elementary school and picture a Parrot/Eagle teacher with an Owl/Dove student. The child never seems to finish her work within the allotted class time. From art projects to math tests, this student seeks perfection and resists moving on until everything is flawless. This causes her to run out of time when attempting to complete assignments.

Although the teacher understands that students move at different speeds, he becomes frustrated. From his perspective, the child's grades do not reflect her capabilities. The teacher becomes impatient with the student and constantly pressures her to move faster. The student begins to internalize her self-perceived inadequacy and loses confidence in her abilities.

Just as teachers may not realize that they impose their personality on students, we may do the same thing to our peers. While we cannot stop others from trying to change us, we can become aware of the expectations we hold for our siblings, roommates and friends. Notice when you expect people to adapt to what *you* want and how *you* would approach a situation.

For example, a Dove may prefer to have a relaxing evening in deep conversation rather than engage in small talk at a party with lots of strangers. His Parrot friend pressures the Dove to go to the party with statements like, "It's no big deal. Just talk with people."

For the Dove, it is a big deal as it makes him feel uncomfortable and bad about himself.

Note the subtle messages you convey to the people you care about most. Do you expect your friends to act in ways that are unnatural to them? Or, do you honor their natural approach to the world? If they want something different than you, do you accept that they have different needs? Or, do you get annoyed and judge them? Be careful about the subtle messages you send to people around you. Welcome friends to be who they are.

- CONSIDER HOW YOU WOULD FEEL if someone tried to change you.

- PAY ATTENTION TO YOUR THOUGHTS. Do you judge what others do as good or bad, right or wrong? Accept that there may be more than one way to approach issues.

- ESTABLISH REALISTIC EXPECTATIONS of others. Determine whether your expectations are based on your approach to the world and whether you are imposing your style on others.

- FOCUS ON THE POSITIVES. Rather than trying to fix others, put your energy into identifying what you appreciate.

- FOCUS ON YOURSELF. Instead of trying to change something out of your control, focus your energy on what you can control . . . *yourself*.

- ACCEPT YOURSELF FULLY, so that you create the space to accept others.

The Spinning Wind

A cool spring breeze ruffled the feathers of the birds who gathered in the Great Field. Gentle swirls of air harkened them back to what brought them together on this day. Xenia, the wise and all-knowing chameleon, scanned the pasture for familiar faces. Ahead of her, sitting quietly on a sizeable boulder, was Simon, a dove whom Xenia had taken under her care.

As Simon's soft, white dove feathers lifted gently in the wind, he smiled at Xenia and her student, Xander, as they approached him. He was happy to see familiar faces during this somber time.

Simon, Xenia, and Xander were three of the many who had gathered to commemorate the tenth anniversary of the Spinning Wind. On that day, a twister tore a path of destruction through the northwest corner of Home and took the lives of two of the land's most beloved parrots.

In a few minutes, the sun would touch the horizon and signal two-minutes of silence in honor of the heroic parrots who lost their lives. Many conversations punctuated the wait. Most were recollections about where someone was and what they were doing when the tragedy occurred.

Xenia made a request. "Xander was not yet born when the Spinning Wind rushed through the forest. Can you tell him about your experiences that day?"

"I'd be glad to," responded Simon, the gentle dove. As he took in a deep breath, a tender breeze stroked him and slightly lifted his wings. Seeing Simon's white feathers standing at attention served to remind his friends of the catastrophe that had destroyed so much of the forest and taken the lives of his friends.

Simon began. "After a long summer vacation, I was back in school. I had just returned home from my third day at Flight School, and I was telling my parents about my new parrot friend, Ivory. I described how different she was from me. She was comical, outgoing, and fun to be with. I had asked my parents if I could play with her, and they agreed. A group of parrots was gathering near the Great Lake, and I went to join them."

"Sounds like a pretty typical day," Xenia said.

"It started out that way," Simon replied. "I was quiet and shy when I was young, so my parents were happy I had made a new friend. They already knew many of the parrots and often called on them. After we arrived at the lake, my parents visited for a time with their adult friends. They told me they were going back home and would come back to pick me up before dinner. With friendly waves and warm glances over their shoulders, my parents left me with Ivory."

"At first, the parrots sounded so noisy. I heard conversations from the adult parrots and cheers from the young parrots, who were joyfully engaged in a crazy game. I was astounded as I watched the youngsters energetically dive-bombing the lake with pine cones. It was pretty funny," Simon smiled in remembrance.

"The parrots sure know how to have fun," Xenia agreed.

"It didn't take long for us to realize that something was wrong. Suddenly, the sky turned dark—very dark. It transformed from a promising blue into an ominous greenish-black shade unlike any I had ever seen before."

"I recall that sky as well," Xenia added. "Then what happened?"

"Unexpectedly, we were pelted with giant balls of solid ice falling from the sky. We all flew for cover. When one of the pieces of ice hit me, it hurt. I was smaller than the parrots, so that one ice ball knocked me right over. When I tried to stand up again, I felt dizzy, and everything in my view went blurry."

"The next thing I remember, I was being sheltered somewhere dark and enclosed. At first, I thought I was dreaming, but when I felt the bump on my head, I realized someone had carried me into a tree hollow. My friend Ivory was with me, and we huddled together. That's when the forest grew as silent as a void. There was a great emptiness. I did not even hear the constant and familiar rustle of leaves. But the stillness was short-lived. That temporary quiet space was merely the forest inhaling deeply in preparation of the devastating wind about to rip through Home.

"Then the forest began to roar. At first it sounded like a few growling bears. But it grew louder and louder until the low rumble turned into a mighty howl. We were puzzled. We didn't know what the sound was. The reverberation increased in intensity until it resembled the bellow of a long, loud waterfall, but that didn't make sense to either of us. Was it a massive swarm of angry bees? That didn't seem right either."

"In those initial moments we were all confused," the chameleon confirmed. "None of us had ever experienced anything like this phenomenon, so we had no frame of reference to work from."

"It was scary," the dove admitted. "But it soon got even scarier. A wall of dirt mixed with dry, dead leaves barreled through the forest. We could hardly see anything. We didn't know where our parents were, and we felt alone. Next, a massive spiral wind began twisting its way through the forest. We heard some trees crashing as they were ripped from the earth. Others were tossed throughout the forest like twigs. Small branches were torn from big trunks, and they slammed into the trees surrounding us. There was so much noise and so much flying debris that we just covered our heads and waited for it to pass. Even though the storm lasted only a few minutes, it felt to us that it would go on forever."

"Fortunately, you were inside a strong tree," Xenia said.

"We were. One of the parrots who did not survive the Spinning Wind had the foresight to place us there. We owe her our lives," said the dove.

"It all sounds so frightening," Xenia said.

"Very," Simon acknowledged. "When the storm passed and I poked my head out of the tree, I saw dark, low-flying clouds overhead. Again, we suffered through an uneasy silence. No one dared make a sound. Even the trees appeared frozen in place. I had never felt anything like what we experienced that day. After a few minutes of stillness, the sun broke through the murky clouds and the branches once again swayed lightly in the breeze. It was as if nothing distressing had happened. Everyone shouted to everyone else, trying to confirm that friends and relatives were all right."

"You survived," affirmed Xenia.

"I did. But Home lost two great friends that day."

"Yes, we did."

"I was amazed at how the surviving parrots responded to the tragedy," Simon stated. "At the same time they were mourning the loss of their loved ones, they were radiating with the optimism that Home would recover soon."

"Hopefulness is a gift the parrots bring to the world," Xenia affirmed.

"Yes. I wish I had some of that," Simon said softly. "The eagles impressed me too."

"How so?" asked the chameleon.

"As soon as the wind died down, the eagles took charge. They rose above the chaos that ensued and immediately jumped into action to make sure everyone was safe."

Xenia smiled. "Eagles handle crises well. In fact, they shine brightest when things are turned upside down."

"I'm not good at that," Simon added.

"Everyone played a role in the aftermath of the Spinning Wind," Xenia noted.

"They did," said Simon. "I remember watching in awe as the owls organized everything with peak efficiency. They thrived on figuring out the complex steps required to return Home to order."

"It was a marvel to behold," Xenia stated.

"I don't know how they do that," said Simon.

"We each have unique gifts," responded Xenia.

"I get that," said the dove. "I just don't understand how something that is so easy for someone else is so difficult for me."

"The reverse is also true. What is easy for you may be difficult for others. I remember watching you in action after the Spinning Wind. You and your family provided comfort to those who had lost their homes. Even though you were young, you listened empathetically to your friends who were impacted by the damage. You selflessly offered your time and energy to help clean up the mess left by the wind. You added stability and consistency at a time when nothing was certain. Others could not have given what you shared so effortlessly."

"But what I did was easy. What they did took skill," Simon replied.

"What they did was easy for them because they were using their natural gifts. What you did was easy for you because you were using yours. Just because what you did was easy for you, doesn't mean that it was less important. Do not devalue your gifts simply because they come easily to you."

Simon took a moment to consider Xenia's words. He had never thought of what he contributed as being special or unique.

Xenia continued. "Did the eagles find it difficult to kick into action and take charge?"

"I don't think so," Simon answered.

"Did the owls find it challenging to create a detailed plan out of nothing?"

"No. In fact, they seemed to enjoy it," answered Simon.

"Precisely!" Xenia declared.

"Do you think it was grueling for the parrots to look on the bright side following the crisis?"

"No. Parrots are eternal optimists. They always find the bright side," said Simon.

"You see," the chameleon explained, "our gifts are easy for us to express. We assume that if they are easy for us, they will be easy for others as well. But that is not the case."

Before beginning the moment of silence designed to honor their lost friends, Xenia offered Simon one final thought: "Value who you are instead of dwelling on what you are not. Self-acceptance is the first step toward releasing the power of your special gifts."

As the forest fell silent, Simon pondered, "When my time in this forest is over, I want to be remembered for how I shared my gifts. I guess the first step is to identify what they are."

Chameleon Wisdom

Wanting to be someone else is a waste of the person you are.
—MARILYN MONROE

In *The Spinning Wind,* Simon admires how the eagles, parrots, and owls responded to the crisis. At the same time, he downplays his own contribution. He does not understand the role he plays in the community and fails to acknowledge his own gifts and contributions.

It is easy for us to look at others and wish we could do what they do. It is more difficult to look at ourselves and appreciate our own abilities.

Before we can get to a place where we accept ourselves fully, we must know ourselves. To know yourself is a lifelong journey of self-exploration. By reading this book, you are already walking down that path.

Getting to know yourself means looking inside and examining your strengths and weaknesses, your likes and dislikes, your habits and idiosyncrasies. Self-knowledge means recognizing your fears and motivations, your feelings and thoughts, your passions and moods.

Once you deepen your understanding of your nature, it is time to accept yourself unconditionally. Self-acceptance is about looking inside, avoiding external distractions, living in the present moment, and owning your failures and successes. When you unconditionally accept who you are, you create the space for growth and joy.

Conversely, self-acceptance does not mean resigning yourself to the hand that has been dealt you. It does not mean ceasing to strive for personal development. It's not about what you did or did not do, or what you wish you were capable of doing.

When a talent is a natural expression of who we are, we think anyone can do it because for us it is easy. We all have abilities that require minimal effort, and these represent our strengths. However, we place more value on the things we work harder to accomplish. We think, "If I don't work for it, it's not valuable." Think about how rewarding your life would be if you valued your natural abilities. The higher the level of self-acceptance you achieve, the more happiness and abundance you can manifest.

Consider a scenario in which an office owl is presented with an exciting new opportunity by a parrot coworker. The parrot is enthusiastic about the possibilities, but all the analytical owl can see are potential obstacles and challenges. A series of worst-case scenarios flood the owl's mind, which causes him to launch a barrage of concerns at the parrot. The parrot leaves the conversation with a list of questions she has been tasked to answer. She is feeling deflated by her interaction with the owl.

Meanwhile, the owl feels better now that the idea will be carefully evaluated. He feels bad, though, that he had to burst the parrot's bubble, and he judges himself disapprovingly for having done so. Further, he wishes that he could be as happy as the parrot and not have to worry about all the things that could go wrong.

Unconditional self-acceptance means embracing the things you like about yourself and the things you do not. In the previous paragraph, the owl made a great contribution to the process, but rather than valuing his own input, he became envious of abilities he did not have. When we embrace ourselves fully, we free ourselves from the need to be accepted by others. This allows our gifts to shine through as we aspire to be the best we can be.

Your worth is not based on a degree that you hold, your performance at work, what your children have accomplished, awards you have won, a title you have earned, the things you own, the money you make, or anything else outside of you. Your self-worth is based on your level of self-acceptance. Self-acceptance is a verb. It is something you do.

The challenges you face are not character defects. There is no such thing as a character defect. Celebrate your strengths and avoid making comparisons with others.

Who you think you are creates your identity. Who you think you are not creates your limitations.

The Chameleon Student

In high school and college, you will encounter people from all walks of life. They will have different interests, backgrounds and personalities. You will see people, most likely Parrots, who effortlessly make new friends. Within weeks, it will seem like they know everyone. You sign up for a sport and it won't take long before one of your teammates, probably an Eagle, has emerged as a natural leader. Some of your fellow students will study calmly for finals with a detailed plan to ensure that they review all the material. These Owls will make it seem effortless. And when one of your friends is dealing with a difficult breakup, a Dove will know exactly what to say and how to provide comfort.

It is only human to watch others with awe and a bit of jealousy when they do things that would be difficult for us to do. "Why can't I do that?" you wonder. As you marvel at their abilities, your friends reflect your perceived inadequacies. You may think that you are not as capable as they are, or that they are better prepared to handle life's challenges. They are not. When they look at you, they are impressed by your innate abilities. Like a mirror, you reflect their perceived weaknesses back at them. This cycle is not healthy for anyone.

We often discount our strengths because they come easily. Instead, we focus on the things that are difficult for us. So, Eagles, don't feel threatened that Parrots can energize the team with their enthusiasm. Appreciate your natural aptitude for managing difficult situations. Parrots, it's okay that you don't organize your time like an Owl! Revel in your ability to see the bright side of any situation. Doves, it is difficult to say "no" when people ask for your time, but that is nothing to beat yourself up about. Appreciate the compassion you bring to the world. And Owls, don't criticize yourself for struggling to give an impromptu speech to a large group. Value your ability to work carefully through complex problems and find the perfect solution.

Appreciate your innate skills as much as you value other people's abilities. Your natural gifts will be the secret to your success in life.

- CONSIDER SELF-ACCEPTANCE as a skill that can be nurtured.

- FORGIVE YOURSELF for not being able to do what others can do. You have strengths that others wish they had.

- SILENCE THE INNER CRITIC. Identify and challenge negative thoughts by replacing them with positive ones.

- LET GO OF PAST REGRETS about things you wish you had done.

- IF YOU WISH TO DEVELOP A CERTAIN SKILL, imagine already having the skill.

- DON'T FOCUS ON WHAT YOU CANNOT DO. Celebrate what you can do.

The Crystal Cave

Two longtime friends, Simon, the dove, and Carl, the owl, sat together enjoying the melodious sounds and dazzling sights of spring. They were delighted by the antics of a group of lively chipmunks who were scurrying back and forth across the forest floor. As the two friends watched the chipmunks invent game after playful game, they were impressed by their neighbors' natural creativity.

Spring, the season of inspiration and expression, was evident in the new life blossoming all around them. Myriad flowers added a variety of vivid colors and fragrant scents to the forest. The trees gave birth to budding leaves, which transformed the warming woodlands from neutral browns into artful greens. The air echoed with the sounds of countless newborns. Simon and Carl felt happy as they sat basking in nature's glory.

Simon and Carl met every Friday morning to enjoy each other's company and talk about life's events. Sometimes, their parrot friend, Ivory, joined them, but she could not make it today. Simon shared how the doves were decorating their family tree with rich and seasonal yellows, reds, and violets. Carl described with precision an invention that he and some other owls were working on, a new weather device that would measure wind speed and provide data on the severity of oncoming storms.

After a few more minutes of enjoying the scene provided by the scampering chipmunks, Simon said, "Ivory would love watching these guys. They are so funny."

"Yes, she would," Carl replied. "Now that I think about it, I have not seen her in days."

"Me neither. I wonder what she's been up to."

The chipmunks scattered hastily as Dee, the eagle, landed in the center of the clearing where the chipmunks had just been playing.

"I'm beginning to think they don't like me," Dee laughed, as she looked up at her two friends.

"I am not sure I blame them," Carl yelled down to Dee. "Eagles and chipmunks are not typically the best of friends."

"I heard what you two were both talking about as I was approaching. Are you looking for Ivory?" the eagle asked directly.

"Yes, we are," Carl replied.

Dee's head turned quickly to the right when she thought she saw a chipmunk run by. "I spotted Ivory flying southeast this morning. She was heading toward Crystal Falls."

"My, that's so far away," Simon gasped. "Was she alone?"

"I didn't see anyone else with her," Dee answered.

"This is quite puzzling," the owl said.

Dee became distracted by a chipmunk who had poked his head out of a hole at the base of a nearby tree. The eagle walked over to the tree and peeked her head into the hole, but she didn't see anything. She looked back to where the little creature had just been, but once again was at a loss. After a few moments of searching, Dee looked up and said, "Hey, I'm going in that direction. Want to join me? We'll see if together we can find Ivory."

"I, for one, would like to find some clues and solve this mystery," Carl stated.

"I don't want to intrude on her private business," Simon added, "but I don't suppose it would hurt anyone to fly out there and see what's happening."

With a powerful thrust of her wings, Dee was airborne. She glanced back over her shoulder with a look that said "follow me."

It took a minute for the dove and the owl to catch up with the eagle, who had slowed down to wait for her friends. Soon the three birds were flying high above Home. Dee was in front. She was followed by Carl, who was flying just off of the eagle's right wing tip. He was trying to find a way to reduce the wind resistance for his friend, Simon, like the geese do, but he couldn't quite get the hang of it. Simon flew right behind Carl.

The trio followed the river below as it snaked its way through the fresh vegetation. The thick smell of spring filled the air as the birds scanned the trees for Ivory. If she were sitting in a tree, she would be easy to spot because of her bright red, yellow, and green feathers. But if she were sitting on the ground, finding her would be more challenging.

Suddenly, Carl was struck by a bright light that bounced off of something below him. At first, he thought it was a reflection of the sun shining on the cascading waters of Crystals Falls, so he didn't mention it. Then, he saw it again. "I see something. Look over there," he pointed.

"I don't see anything," Simon said.

"Me neither," Dee concurred.

All of a sudden, a blinding, bright yellow ray of light caught their eyes. This time they all saw what it was.

"Let's go," Dee instructed, as she took a sharp turn and dove to the right. She was heading directly for the light, and Carl was right behind her.

Simon's eyes grew wide. "We don't know what's down there. Are you sure we should . . ."

As the eagle and the owl bolted straight to the flash, Simon turned to join his friends. He landed on a branch high above the river, which was being fed by the waters of the tumbling waterfall. The dove recognized this place; his parents had brought him here when he was just a little bird. Simon remembered the wisdom his father had imparted to him long ago. "These falls hide a great secret," his father had said. "Behind that rushing waterfall is the Crystal Cave. It is filled with gems of all shapes and sizes—red rubies, purple amethysts, green emeralds, yellow citrine, orange sunstone, clear quartz, and more." Then he said something about a magic egg-shaped rock.

As Simon approached his friends, he noticed they were gazing at the ground beside the falls. From up high, the dove could only see waterfall mist blowing in the wind. But when he landed, he could not believe his eyes. Simon looked at Carl who was looking at Dee who was looking at Simon.

"What on earth?" Carl asked.

"How stunning!" Simon exclaimed.

"I've never seen anything so creative," added Dee.

The trio stared in amazement at the exquisite work of art that adorned the land below them.

A burst of color erupted out of the center of the falls. It was Ivory! She was carrying a long piece of orange citrine, and its vivid gold form was reflecting off the water. The parrot didn't seem to notice her friends as she set herself down next to an elaborate maze of twinkling, multicolored gems. She studied her artwork a bit before deciding to move some items around.

First, she picked up a dozen small, red stones and used them to encircle a long, clear piece of quartz. Next, she took three quartz crystals, each slightly bigger than her parrot frame, and stood them vertically in a line. She then shifted her attention to a royal-purple amethyst. She moved it onto a large slab of white selenite, where it rested peacefully. Her rearrangement had made room for her to place her new specimen, the citrine.

"Wonderful, isn't it?" said a soft, low voice from just behind the trio.

The three friends immediately recognized the voice. "Over here," called their mentor, Xenia. The birds turned toward the voice, but the chameleon had already slithered across a long branch to rest just above them.

"Quite astonishing, is it not?" the chameleon asked.

"It's so lively and colorful," Carl said, "but it is so . . . um . . . well . . ."

"Abstract?" the chameleon offered.

"Exactly!" the owl replied. "It is quite creative. I could never do anything like that. But there is no order to it."

"Yet it is still beautiful," the chameleon affirmed.

The structured owl tried to make sense of what he was seeing. "I am not saying it is not beautiful. I just do not understand how she could have conceived of something like that, let alone constructed it without a plan. Does she have an objective for this project?"

Xenia smiled.

Simon interjected, "I think Carl is saying that Ivory is so imaginative, and the rest of us just don't think like that."

"So you are not creative either?" Xenia asked.

"Not really," Simon conceded. "I'd like to be, but I never have been."

"Fascinating," replied Xenia. She then shifted her perceptive eyes to Dee. "And how about you, my eagle friend? Are you creative?"

"Well, I do have a lot of ideas, but I'm too busy to explore them. So I guess not."

"If I understand the three of you correctly, Ivory is the only creative one among you?" Xenia probed.

"Seems that way," Dee confirmed.

Xenia looked down at the glowing mandala of gems. She then glanced back at the trio and stated, "Everyone is creative, but each of us expresses creativity differently."

"But look at that," Carl suggested. "I could never do that."

Xenia replied, "If you judge your creativity based on the works of others, you will inevitably perceive yourself as inadequate."

Carl looked down at the glowing gems, then back at Xenia. "I have never considered myself to be creative because I am such a perfectionist. It is hard to be original when I am always caught up in details."

"Carl, that is precisely what makes you so inventive," answered Xenia. "You examine the world around you from so many perspectives, and that skill enables you to embrace complex problems. Take a look at your crafting hobbies. You can focus for hours on solving an issue when others would have given up long before you. And when you create something, you make sure it is precisely the way you want it. I remember the intricate welcome sign you crafted. You used materials in ways I had never imagined before. It must have taken you weeks to prepare each component of the sign before you began construction."

"Actually, it took months," Carl said.

"I have no idea how you managed to curve the outer branches on the frame of that the sign. That was so inventive," complimented Xenia.

"I used steam from the hot springs. It took a while," explained Carl.

"The sign is so ornate. I marvel at your creation," Xenia said.

"If I am being honest," Carl admitted, "it has a few mistakes in it."

"When I look at it," Xenia said, "I see how much time and attention you put into every aspect of the sign. And those 'mistakes' aren't mistakes. They are, instead, part of the sign's charm."

"Well, thank you," Carl responded.

Ivory popped out of the falls again. This time she was carrying a dark-burgundy garnet. The group watched as she shifted a few other stones to make room for the new arrival.

The chameleon looked deeply into Simon's eyes and shared, "You display creativity as well. Have you ever noticed how you bring harmony to the world around you? You always know how to bring others together and make them feel comfortable. You figure out how to say things in just the right way."

"But that's not me being creative. That's just me being me," Simon suggested, downplaying Xenia's compliment.

Xenia laughed. "Simon, my friend, when you express yourself creatively, it feels easy because it's natural for you. Look how you decorated your home. You have created an inviting place for everyone who visits. You make meals that delight your guests, and you are a warm and wonderful host. When you see others engaged in a conflict, you find a creative way to bring those who were estranged back together again."

"I never thought of that as creativity," Simon acknowledged.

"Well, it is," Xenia affirmed. "Remember the day you put yourself right in the middle of that battle between two rabbits? They were talking too quickly and not listening to each other. I will never forget what you did."

"You saw that?" Simon asked.

"I watched you feed one of the rabbits a mixture of carrots and maple sap. While he was eating, you asked the other rabbit to share what was bothering her. Since the first couldn't talk while he was eating, he was finally able to hear what was upsetting the other. You then offered the second rabbit your sticky mixture, and while she was eating, the first one shared his concerns. Within a few minutes, you mediated a battle that had been raging for days. You figured out how to get the two rabbits to listen to each other and resolve their differences. It was brilliant! Pure creativity in action!"

"Thank you, Xenia," said Simon. "You're very kind."

Dee straightened up a little because she knew she was going to be next. "Before you say anything about me," stated Dee, "I'd like to retract my previous statement that I am not creative."

"So you now see yourself as creative?" Xenia asked.

"Not exactly, but I think you are about to tell me that I am creative, and I don't like being wrong," Dee laughed.

"You are never wrong!" Xenia jested. "But sometimes you aren't always completely right."

"I'll accept that," the eagle chuckled. "So how do you see my creativity?"

"You can create something out of nothing. You see the world from 10,000 feet above, and you don't get caught up in the minutiae. You challenge yourself to achieve new heights. And when you offer solutions, you decisively break free of old patterns and ways of thinking."

Dee immediately understood what Xenia was saying, even though she, too, had not previously considered herself to be creative. She just thought that how she acted was how it should be done.

The group silently watched Ivory as she continued to reorganize the gems. The parrot picked up one stone and moved it. She took a few steps back to review the design and then moved that same stone again. Ivory disappeared into the cave for a few minutes and emerged with something new. She didn't seem to have a plan, yet she worked quickly and with purpose.

After watching Ivory repeat her pattern several times, Xenia noted, "Ivory is in *the zone*. She has no sense of time while she is creating. Her inspiration flows from her intuition, and even though she can get quite excited about her ideas, she has no attachment to them."

"I guess I've been thinking about creativity all wrong," Simon said contemplatively. "It's not a question of whether or not we are creative. It's a question of how we express our creativity. We are all creative."

Xenia grinned and said, "My work here is done." And with that, she harmonized her coloring with the branch she was sitting on and faded into the assorted shades of the forest.

The three friends watched Ivory's artistic efforts for a while longer and then decided to leave her to her work. As they headed home, they talked about the unique and interesting ways they each expressed themselves.

Chameleon Wisdom

Everybody is talented because everybody who is human has something to express.
—Brenda Ueland

We were all born creative. Along the way, however, many of us have convinced ourselves that we were not. Think back to your childhood. It's a safe bet that you built sand castles, played with Legos, created Popsicle-stick art, served plastic food to imaginary people, and invented new games.

When you hand crayons to children, they start drawing. They don't say, "I'm not creative." Some children draw a sun surrounded by alternating short and long yellow rays. Other children's suns wear a face. Still others are colored purple. Yet all are created freely, without judgment.

As we get older, people buy into the societal belief that creativity must be spontaneous, bold, and original. We have been taught that creativeness resides exclusively in the domain of artists, crafters, writers, musicians, and performers. If you don't fall into one of those categories, you probably have assumed, by default, you are not creative. It's as if someone has told you along the way that you are not creative, and you have accepted the idea as reality.

In *The Crystal Cave*, Dee, Simon, and Carl were impressed by Ivory's creativity. They marveled at what she was capable of doing while, simultaneously, downplaying their own creative abilities.

They defined "creativity" in a way that did not match their own gifts. They believed that only someone with a different style than theirs could be creative.

We all live in a constant state of creativity, but because it is not conscious, we discount it. How we think, react, solve problems, and approach the world defines our creative expression. Yet many of us are not in touch with our creative gifts, so we don't see ourselves in that light.

Creativity can take many forms. Each is driven by our personality style. When we are "in the zone," we display originality and inventiveness because the comfort of using our style-driven strengths frees us to take risks and express freely. Consider the creative power of each of the four styles:

Eagles: These paradigm shifters think out of the box, reject existing assumptions, and display revolutionary thinking. Eagles see possibilities where others see obstacles. They see rules as a problem, and they do not feel bound by artificial constraints. Eagles prefer working on challenges at their inception, where boundary-breaking thinking takes place, rather than at the more structured implementation phases of ideas. They tend to be independent problem solvers and do not need consensus to move forward. In fact, others not recognizing the merits of their ideas spur them to push even harder. Eagles are creative at figuring out ways to make things happen and get results.

Parrots: The parrots are idea factories; they solve problems intuitively. They create innovative ideas out of nothingness. They represent what many people typically define as a "creative" person. Parrots find new uses for existing objects and combine things in ways that others do not consider. Since they generate a lot of ideas that aren't always based on a significant amount of thought, they are not overly vested in their ideas. And why should they be? To parrots, there's always another idea on the way. Parrots tend to have proverbial "Eureka" moments. Like eagles, they prefer not to focus on the details required to bring an idea to life.

Doves: Doves are stabilizers who transform disorder into harmony. Instead of developing completely new systems, they work creatively within existing frameworks and systems. Novelty is not a requirement for the creativity doves share with the world. They tap into the knowledge, skills, and abilities of others; utilize structures; and convert them into something new. Doves are comfortable with solutions in which everyone agrees with the process and result. Doves enjoy hobbies like scrapbooking or fashioning family photo albums. They enjoy working with others during the creative process and do not tend to recognize themselves as creative, despite the deeply personal innovative style they express.

Owls: Owls bring structure and order to the world around them. Their creations can be highly complex, requiring patience and an eye for detail. Sometimes their creativity evolves from asking such questions as "why" and "what if." Their ideas come from a deep examination of the possibilities based on data and knowledge. They consider many options before acting. Owls have insight into highly specialized areas, and they do not share their ideas until they have been properly vetted and can be well-articulated. Owls can become consumed by analyzing ideas and producing perfection, but they sometimes get stuck when it comes to implementing these ideas.

When we appreciate the differences in creative approaches, we can recognize and tap into our own natural talent. The only difference between creative people and uncreative people is that creative people understand how to express their creativity.

The Chameleon Student

Our school years offer many opportunities to express creativity. In the classroom, our personalities shine through every project and presentation. How we play sports, make friends and approach classwork reflects who we are.

The key is to engage our innate forms of creativeness. If you're a Parrot, find ways to infuse Parrot charisma into group projects. If you're an Owl, don't try to be a Parrot. That would be exhausting. Use your analytical abilities to gain a deep understanding of the content of your assignments. This will empower you to question assumptions and thereby explore new possibilities. If you're an Eagle, you likely have big-picture vision and want to do things differently than anyone who has come before you. Challenge your group to seek novel solutions rather than resort to the conventional approach. If you're a Dove, inspire creativity by fostering teamwork and collaboration.

We are all creative, but personality affects how we express our innovative ideas. If you take on responsibilities that fit your style, your creativity will shine brightly.

However, as a freshman or as a new club member, you may find fewer opportunities to express creativity in a way that embodies your style. This might happen for a few reasons. In school, you must take required courses that may not relate to your interests or desired career. But after you complete your prerequisites, you will be free to take courses that excite you and fit your style. Creativity is likely to flow when who you are matches what you choose to learn.

In extracurricular activities, younger students may have to 'pay their dues' before earning a position that reflects their personality. In those early years, routine tasks may not provide room for ingenuity. This is what happens at work too. At first, we follow the process and do things the way they were taught to us. As we work our way up in the organization, opportunities to display ingenuity become abundant.

One day, when you are in a job that embraces your personality, creativity will flow effortlessly. It may take a little while to get there, but hang in there. Before you know it, you will have a job that resonates with who you are.

- KNOW THAT YOU ARE CREATIVE. Even if you feel you haven't created anything in a while, you are more imaginative than you think you are. The capacity for creativity resides within you.

- DON'T LET OTHERS DEFINE WHAT CREATIVITY means to you. Define it for yourself.

- RECOGNIZE HOW YOU CHANNEL your creative energy.

- IDENTIFY AND ALTER disempowering beliefs about your creativity.

- DO THINGS THAT INSPIRE YOU, and share your creativity with the world.

Hatching Day Surprise

Spring was the time to revel in all of life's glory. Almost daily the birds celebrated Hatching Day parties for the older residents of Home who were being acknowledged for the first day they felt the warmth of the sun.

When Ivory stopped by to visit her friend Carl, she was hiding something—but Carl was none the wiser. Ivory and the rest of her parrot friends were organizing a Surprise Hatching Day party for the owl, and it was Ivory's job to keep him busy and nowhere near the location of the big event.

After convincing Carl to join her on some errands, the two birds made their way to the Lost Bird Department, where Ivory dropped off a job application. When they arrived, Carl asked, "Isn't today the deadline?"

"Yes, it is," Ivory answered.

"You waited until the day it was due to submit it?" questioned Carl.

"It's not late" Ivory answered, a bit confused. "What's the problem?"

Carl shook his head. He couldn't imagine waiting until the due date to drop off an application.

The two friends traveled north to the amphitheater at the base of Xanadu's peak. Ivory delivered several scrolls that contained costume designs for the upcoming play. Carl wondered what play they were going to put on, but Ivory only would reveal something about a groundhog and some wings. "You're going to love it!" she promised the owl.

The pair then made their way to the Great Field, where Ivory dropped off vines and twigs that she had been gathering on their journey. When Ivory handed the bundle to a blue-and-yellow parrot, she said with a big grin, "My *hat* comes off to you, dear sir. It is an *honor* to bring these sticks to you."

When Carl asked what she was talking about, Ivory avoided the question by pretending to be distracted. The owl didn't give Ivory's diverted attention another thought because her focus was often pulled in different directions.

The friends spent a pleasant day together wandering throughout Home. They stopped to visit a few eagles, shared some information with several parrots, and picked up some food that had been prepared by a family of doves. Ivory kept Carl busy while their party friends got ready for the big gathering. The plan had worked perfectly.

As the sun neared the horizon, Ivory informed Carl they had to make one last stop.

"Where are we headed this time?" Carl questioned. He was getting tired of covering so much distance. He thought they could have been much more efficient. He would have mapped out all of the stops before they began.

"My father asked me to go to the Council Tree to deliver a message. It won't take long," Ivory assured him.

By this point, Carl had resigned himself to the fact that Ivory was not going to provide specifics, and even though it went against his nature, he went along for the ride. When they landed on an outstretched branch at the far end of the Council Tree, nobody else was there.

"This is odd," Carl observed. "Where is everyone? There's always someone . . ."

Ivory interrupted her friend. "I've got something to tell you."

Without warning, more than fifty of Carl's friends burst forth from behind the trunks of the trees and shouted, "SURPRISE!"

Carl jumped. His heart skipped a beat. It took a moment for him to regain his breath. He was not a fan of the unexpected. He looked around and noticed that all eyes were aimed on him, and he didn't know what to say. He hesitated then stuttered, "Uh . . . um . . . what are all of you doing here?"

He turned to Ivory and whispered, "You shouldn't have."

"Oh, get out," Ivory laughed. "Of course I should have. You're a great friend and you deserve this celebration."

"I deserve this?" Carl mumbled to himself. "What did I do to deserve this?"

From a higher branch, the blue-and-yellow parrot they met earlier bestowed Carl with what he called "The Hatching Day Hat of Honor." The parrot was so excited to place the hat on Carl's head. He had worked hard to weave thick, brown vines together to form a ring. From the center of the hat rose a large, colorful arrow pointing straight down to Carl. The owl couldn't have felt more ridiculous.

One by one, Carl's friends approached to wish him a Happy Hatching Day. Carl felt trapped. This was *not* his idea of fun.

A little while later, a large purple-and-red parrot rapidly approached Carl and said, "Come with me. I want to show you something!"

The owl could not imagine what new horror awaited him. The pair flew to a neighboring tree and Carl saw a mouse-shaped cake topped with candles. *Things are shaping up*, Carl thought.

Then another parrot rushed over and said, "I found your hat. It must have fallen off."

"Oh, great," Carl replied through a forced smile, as he placed the hat back on his head. The group then sang a rousing rendition of "You Got that Right, You're My Favorite Owl."

The song transitioned the party to the highlight of the evening, at least from the parrots' perspective. The entire group of birds was summoned to a high branch overlooking Home. One of the parrots introduced what she called "Canyon Karaoke." This involved singing a song as loudly as possible so that it echoed off the canyon wall in the distance.

When nobody was looking, Carl quietly escaped to talk privately with Simon, his longtime dove friend. For the first time since the party began, Carl felt comfortable.

Later that evening, after most of the guests had cleared out, Carl and Ivory sat quietly on a large branch away from the center of the action. "Can I take this off now?" Carl asked, looking up toward his hat.

"Sure. It's yours. You can do anything you want with it," Ivory replied.

Carl removed the hat and looked thoughtfully into the distance. Ivory broke the silence. "I'll bet you were surprised."

"Oh, you can say that again," Carl stammered.

Sensing some hesitation in his voice, Ivory asked, "Didn't you like the party?"

With practiced diplomacy, Carl replied, "It was a nice gesture."

"But didn't you enjoy it?" Ivory asked with astonishment.

"Well, I am not accustomed to being the center of attention."

"Why not?" she asked. "It's your special day."

"I do not know how to react. It is uncomfortable for me."

Ivory felt bad. "I didn't mean to make you feel uncomfortable. I love parties, and, I must admit, I enjoy the attention. I figured you would, too."

"I know you meant well. And it was nice to see everyone." Carl stated as he looked off into the distance. "This reminds me of something that Xenia once shared with us. She told me that we often expect others to like what we like and want what we want."

"I remember that day," Ivory said. "And if I recall correctly, Xenia also said that if we only consider our own desires when we try to please others, we honor who *we* are, not who *they* are."

Ivory looked down at the hat. "I guess what we're saying here is that if it were me, I would have enjoyed a surprise party to celebrate my Hatching Day. I assumed you would, too."

"That is not an unreasonable assumption," Carl acknowledged. "Truth be told, I would never have thrown a party for you because I would not have wanted one myself."

"So you're not throwing me a party for my next Hatching Day?" Ivory joked.

"Well, now that I realize that I need to consider what you like as opposed to what I like, one never knows what lies ahead."

"Oh, a mystery. I like that!" Ivory grinned. "And for the record, I wouldn't mind a Hatching Day Hat of Honor."

Chameleon Wisdom

*Do not do unto others as you
expect they should do unto you.
Their tastes may not be the same.*
—George Bernard Shaw

We've all heard the Golden Rule, also known as the Ethic of Reciprocity, "Treat others how you want to be treated." This guideline for how we should treat other people exists in many religions and cultures throughout history and across the globe.

This moral truth is most notably applied to virtues such as kindness, respect, and honesty. For example, if I want you to be kind to me, I should be kind to you. If I want you to respect me, I should respect you. And if I want you to be honest with me, I should be honest with you. It's hard to argue with such a time-tested principle that is so universally accepted. The Golden Rule puts your own needs in the spotlight, and this is perfectly acceptable when applied to virtues.

However, this maxim does not work in every situation, especially those in which we have needs that are based on our own style. What if someone has a different style than you do and their needs are not the same as yours? If you treat others how *you* want to be treated, you will be honoring your style, not theirs.

There is another principle that takes the style of others into account, and it is based on the notion that the opposite of profound wisdom is often more profound wisdom. In this case, the inverse of the Golden Rule—referred to in *Taking Flight!* as the Home Rule—states, "Treat others how *they* need to be treated, not how *you* need to be treated." The Home Rule is based on the premise that we all have different needs. Therefore, the Home Rule requires energy, empathy, and insight.

Overall, we tend to treat others how *we* like to be treated, not how *they* like to be treated. We saw this play out in *Hatching Day Surprise* when Ivory mistakenly assumed that Carl would enjoy a surprise party because she would have enjoyed a surprise party. By inadvertently applying the Golden Rule, the parrot treated the owl how *she* would like to be treated. Had Ivory taken a moment to consider Carl's personality style and needs, she would never have arranged such an event.

Imagine an owl and a parrot as a married couple. The owl spouse has a lot of systems that need to be followed in the household. These systems relate to everything from where shoes should be stored to how the dishwasher should be stacked and the towels should be folded. Now imagine the owl's parrot spouse. The parrot feels that a home should be comfortable and free of constraints. As a result, the parrot feels overwhelmed trying to keep everything in predefined locations all the time.

The owl becomes frustrated with the parrot and proceeds to annoy him with constant nagging. The couple gets stuck in an endless loop of conflict. If we can rise above the discord, it is easy to see what is taking place. The spouses are imposing their own style-driven needs on each other. They are creating an environment that makes themselves feel comfortable without taking into consideration the needs of the other.

This tendency to consider our needs ahead of the needs of others also plays out in the workplace. Consider an eagle manager who leads a group of dove employees. The eagle creates a new process that changes all of their procedures. He informs the doves of the new set of guidelines but provides little information and almost no warning before they take effect. The eagle is excited about the results he expects from the new system, and he assumes the doves will be as well.

After announcing the change, the eagle asks the doves if they have any questions. They do not speak up because they need time to consider the new information. The eagle interprets their silence as acceptance. When it comes time to implement the latest procedures, the doves move slowly to adapt and support them. This frustrates the eagle, who cannot understand their resistance. The eagle treated the doves as if they had eagle-like preferences, and the results will not be optimal for either party.

When you treat others based on your own needs, you convey that you do not care enough about the others to figure out what they want. Applying the Home Rule requires effort. First, you have to recognize your own style and not impose it on others. Second, you have to consider the styles of others so you can meet their needs.

When you make conscious decisions based on who you are *and* who others are, you create the basis for deep and lasting relationships. You are also more likely to get what you want when others get what they want.

The Chameleon Student

It is common to believe that other people like and need the same things we do. And why not? If I like something, why wouldn't you like it too? This faulty assumption can lead to hurt feelings and drama between friends. Living with three or four total strangers (a.k.a. roommates) in college can magnify the potential for conflict.

For instance, imagine an Owl who likes to keep all his belongings and classwork visible and accessible. The room may look messy, but the Owl knows exactly where everything is. This Owl shares a room with a different type of Owl (yes, Owls come in multiple varieties) who likes to organize their belongings and put everything neatly in its predesignated place. Everything is put away immediately after its use. Can you imagine the potential for drama? We assume that others will act as we act, but when they do not, we get frustrated, angry or disappointed.

Visualize a Parrot who likes to keep the dorm-room door open so that a steady stream of friends pop in to say hello. Contrast this with a Dove who prefers a private space where she can study quietly in solitude. People with different personalities can struggle to understand why someone would have different needs than they do. These differences can fuel assumptions of inconsiderateness and indifference because we reason, "Well *I* would never treat someone like that!"

The expectation that others like what we like can also play out in our hobbies too. An Eagle may prefer to go running by himself because he prefers to set his own pace while the solitude clears his head. His Dove friend likes companionship because, in the Dove's experience, people feed off each other's energy and push each other to keep up the pace. The Dove is offended that the Eagle runs alone each morning even though the Dove has expressed interest in joining the Eagle. The Dove may conclude that the Eagle does not like the Dove. In reality, the Eagle considers the Dove to be a close friend, but they have very different needs.

When we accept that different personalities are driven by different needs, frustration fades, judgment disappears and we cultivate stronger relationships. Honor the needs of your friends, and watch how conflicts become rarer and easier to resolve.

- PAY ATTENTION TO HOW OTHERS TREAT YOU. Since we tend to treat others how we need to be treated, the way others treat you is a window into their needs.

- DISPLAY EMPATHY AND COMPASSION. Tune in to the unstated needs of others.

- PRACTICE ACTIVE LISTENING. When you pay attention, you may hear others telling you what they want.

- ASK OTHERS WHAT THEIR NEEDS ARE. The easiest way to identify someone's needs is to ask what they want.

Summer

A Trip to the Beach

For weeks, Ivory had been asking Dee to join her for a weekend adventure at the beach. Ivory planned to kick off the summer with an exciting bang. The journey required nearly half a day's travel, so Dee wasn't sure the strategy of taking a short trip, with only one overnight, would give them enough time to see all the sights. Nevertheless, in order to stop her enthusiastic parrot friend's constant pestering, Dee agreed.

On the morning of their departure, Dee waited for Ivory in her large eagle nest settled high above Home. As the blushing dawn had already transitioned into a stunning blue, Dee was becoming increasingly annoyed. They were supposed to have taken off a while ago, but Ivory was nowhere in sight.

Finally, the parrot's bright colors flashed across the horizon as she leisurely approached Dee's nest. The eagle was tapping her talon impatiently when Ivory swooped in for a landing.

"Sorry I'm late," the parrot apologized.

The eagle sighed. "I thought we were supposed to meet at dawn. We need to get started so we have enough time to explore the beach today."

"I'm ready to go," Ivory announced excitedly. "I would have gotten here sooner, but I saw the most amazing sight—the sun rising over the Great Lake. It was incredible. You should have seen it. The mist was floating on the water, and a bunch of shiny fish were jumping so high they were penetrating the fog. It looked as if they were sailing through clouds. You should have been there."

"Actually, you should have been *here*," Dee stated. "Well, you are here now. Let's get going."

The two birds leapt from the nest and set a course for Sea Turtle Cove. They flew south, over hills that rolled like giant turtle shells and fields filled with salmon and indigo wildflowers. The landscape was stunning, and Ivory was overwhelmed. Once they left their familiar surroundings, Ivory commented on almost everything she saw. "Look at that!" she often exclaimed. "Check that out! Do you see it? Isn't that incredible?"

Ivory's animated commentary continued nonstop for hours. Dee was amazed at how she could carry on a conversation by herself. When Ivory passed a rocky stream, she shared a funny story about something that had happened to her in a rocky stream. When they passed a fallen tree, she shared a story about a fallen tree. It was as if Ivory had an endless reservoir of experiences to call upon. Dee tried hard to listen to the details of Ivory's stories, but often found herself tuning them out.

At one point they came to a towering waterfall, even bigger than Crystal Falls. "Oh, my!" the parrot declared. "We *have* to go see it. It is humongous! I've never seen a waterfall this big before! Have you?"

Before the eagle could answer, Ivory banked right, beelining toward the falls. "Well, I guess we're taking a detour," Dee mumbled.

"Do you believe this?" Ivory asked. "That must be a 1,000-foot drop! This is remarkable!"

"It is *impressive*," Dee agreed.

"I'm going in!" the parrot proclaimed.

"Going in?" the eagle asked. "What do you mean by . . ." but it was too late. Ivory was heading directly toward the falls. Just as she reached the water, she turned a hard left and coasted through the iridescent spray that was the byproduct of the tumbling water.

"Isn't this fantastic?" Ivory yelled.

"Uh, yeah. It's fantastic," Dee replied. "But we've a got a lot of distance to cover, and there are a lot of things to see at the beach. We've got to get going."

After the parrot made a few more passes through the mist, they continued on their way. The next hour or so was filled with waterfall talk. Well, actually, it was filled with Ivory gushing about the waterfall and Dee listening. Somehow, the falls were growing bigger and the danger was becoming more pronounced with each telling of the story.

Next they flew over a dense area of Home filled with mangrove trees that ranged as far as their eyes could see. The groves were framed by a steep cliff rising high into the air. As the two friends increased their altitude to soar above the rock face, Ivory spotted something new.

"What is that?" the parrot inquired as she directed Dee's sharp eagle vision to the center of a rock formation jutting out from the cliff.

"It's a mountain goat," Dee answered. "There are several of them there."

"I've only heard about mountain goats," Ivory said with delight. "We've got to check them out."

Without hesitation, Ivory aimed straight toward the strange and unfamiliar creatures. She landed at the top of a tall pine and shouted to Dee, "Let's watch from here."

Dee settled onto a tree that was not far from their original flight path.

"These guys are hilarious!" Ivory yelled to her friend. "Look how they jump from rock to rock. And if you listen closely, they sound like laughter. It must be fun to be a mountain goat! Isn't it entertaining to watch them butt heads?"

"Butting heads, huh? Don't know what that's like," Dee thought sarcastically. "Now I know why eagles are bald. This parrot is driving me so crazy, I'm going to lose all my feathers by the time this trip is over."

"What was that?" Ivory shouted. "I can't hear you over all the head butting!"

"Nothing!" Dee grimaced. She squirmed for a few minutes until finally stating, "We need to go. We still have a long flight ahead of us, and we don't want to miss anything at the beach."

Ivory stayed for a few more minutes before turning to her friend. "I'm having such a great time on our trip. A sunrise over the lake. Giant waterfalls. Funny mountain goats. Who could ask for anything more?"

The pair continued on as Ivory reflected on her experience with the goats and talked about what she wanted to do when they arrived at Sea Turtle Cove.

After one more detour into a foggy swamp where Ivory thought she spied a double-rainbow, they finally arrived at their destination.

"We're here," Dee declared.

They landed on the dry sand, just out of reach of the ocean waves. Ivory looked out at the red-wine sky stretching across the horizon and asked, "Isn't this beautiful?"

"It is. I just wish we would have gotten here earlier," Dee replied with a hint of annoyance.

"Is something wrong?" Ivory asked. "It sounds like something is bothering you."

"It's just that we took too much time to get here. We should have . . ."

Just then, a large sea turtle floated in on a wave and walked patiently onto the shore. Both birds were both surprised to see it heading their way. When the turtle reached them, she spoke softly and deliberately. "Welcome to Sea Turtle Cove. Consider our beach to be your home away from Home."

The turtle then turned and walked leisurely back to the surf.

"Can you believe it?" Ivory beamed. "That was the oldest sea turtle I've ever seen! She must be a 100 years old!"

"Yes, she must be quite old," Dee replied.

"So what's wrong?" Ivory asked. "Aren't you excited to be here?"

"Yes, I am, but it's already dusk," Dee replied. "We planned to get here earlier, but you kept taking us off course."

Ivory was about to respond when they noticed the turtle making her way back to them. Neither bird said a word. The turtle asked them, "Would you indulge an old turtle such as me to share a few observations?"

Surprised by the turtle's reemergence, they both nodded.

The sea turtle took a slow, deep breath before saying, "Many creatures have crossed my path throughout my lifetime. From the assertive seagull to the playful dolphin . . . from the industrious beaver to the patient snail . . . I have met them all. And if there is one thing I have noticed, it is this: There are many ways to reach a destination, and we usually choose the path that reflects who we are."

The turtle turned to Dee and continued, "As an eagle, you keep your eye on your goal and do not get distracted by what is around you."

"Absolutely," Dee affirmed. "That's how I get things done."

"And your path mirrored your desire to get here quickly," said the sea turtle.

The turtle then turned to Ivory and said, "As a parrot, you enjoy life to its fullest. You take every opportunity to experience whatever presents itself to you. It does not matter if it takes you off course for a little while."

"You got that right," Ivory agreed. "Life is meant to be lived."

"And your journey here reflected the essence of who you are." The old turtle hinted at a smile and asked, "So which way is the right way?"

After pausing to watch a seagull dive into the water and emerge with a fish, the turtle added, "Or should I ask, is there a right way?"

Both birds started to answer in unison, but the turtle interjected. "The answers are not for me. They are for you. I will leave you with this: We tend to stay in our natural style until someone or something pulls us out of it. When that happens, we feel uncomfortable. But make no mistake, that uncomfortable zone is where growth occurs. It is also where adventure resides."

The laid-back sea turtle bowed her head respectfully to the visitors and eased herself into a large incoming wave. As she drifted gently out to sea, she bellowed, "Learn from others, and add these new ways to your own. One day they will serve you well. And say hello to Xenia for me." They watched the sea turtle float effortlessly away, drifting wherever the waves took her.

The pair spent the rest of the day enjoying beach sites. Dee was excited to watch an albatross diving for squid. The eagle was particularly impressed by the albatross's hunting technique. They also got to see a hidden cove that very few before them had explored. Dee and Ivory bravely navigated the tunnel's twists and turns, and they exited feeling exhilarated.

Dee said, "On our trip here, I noticed a cave that might be filled with bats. Want to check it out on our way home tomorrow?"

Ivory grinned, "Sure. But let's not spend too much time there. We don't want to return too late."

Chameleon Wisdom

Growth demands a temporary surrender of security.
—Gail Sheehy

We all have behaviors that are natural and comfortable. These behaviors represent a relaxed *and* energizing place that is based on the bird style that most resembles us. We call our natural state our "style zone."

Working outside of our style zone can feel awkward and exhausting because we are internally battling to return to a place of comfort and security. After being out of our zone for a while, we feel the need to go home, rest, and recharge. We feel as if we need to reset ourselves back to our original factory settings. Our brains are creatures of habit; they prefer to follow well-known and well-worn neural connections. When we move outside of our default approach to solving problems or interacting with others, we feel uneasy. We have no hardwiring for the new behaviors.

The human brain is like a human muscle. When we stretch it, it gets stronger. Each time we try something new, we create fresh neural connections and synapses. When we repeat the process, the new actions become ingrained. This progression expands the outer edges of our range by challenging habits that limit performance.

We spend a good portion of our lives on autopilot, mindlessly living our days without thought or intention. On the positive side, our habits help us successfully engage in familiar tasks without wasting too much brain power or energy. On the negative side, the boundaries of our natural tendencies require a great expenditure of energy in order to expand. Because we often fear that the challenge of acting in new ways will lead to failure, judgment, or rejection, we fall back on a state of complacency.

We all seek to remain in our style zone until someone or something pulls us out of it. In *A Trip to the Beach*, Dee is annoyed that Ivory continually stops to enjoy the sights on the way to their destination. As a parrot, Ivory lives in the moment and thrills at experiencing the many wonders of the forest. As an eagle, Dee is goal directed. She wants to get where they are going and feel as if they have accomplished their goal. Dee becomes frustrated when Ivory pulls her out of her natural style. However, when Dee does open up to new ways of behaving, she creates the potential for deeper and richer experiences. Likewise, Ivory learns from Dee that it's important to remain focused.

When you expand the perimeter of your natural state, you gain confidence and fresh perspectives. You acquire new skills and grow stronger and wiser. You may even inspire those around you to leave the safety of their preset factory settings.

Let's take a look at the typical style zones for each of the birds:

Eagles are willing to try new things if the risk will create a big reward. Eagles are all about the outcome. They will put themselves in a position of discomfort if it is likely to yield a big payoff.

After all, you have to be willing to try something new if you want to go where nobody has gone before. Eagles find it frustrating to slow down and pay attention to the feelings of others when a task needs to be accomplished.

Parrots often seek new and varied activities. They will leave their style zone for the exhilaration of a new experience. Parrots revel in new adventures. And why not? Whatever happens will make a good story to tell. Parrots find it more difficult to spend time creating detailed systems than to simply wing it.

Doves will step out of their safe approach to the world to defend friends or family members who are being treated disrespectfully. While doves dislike confrontation, they will push their boundaries to come to the aid of others. However, doves may have difficulty being assertive and standing up to fight for their own needs.

Owls will leave the clearly defined scope of their style only if it makes logical sense to do so. Before they do, they typically engage in a thorough analysis. When owls finally take the risk of leaving their well-practiced behaviors, hazards are often minimized by careful planning. Owls are uncomfortable when they are placed in the spotlight or in situations that require a significant outward display of emotion.

Recall a moment in your life when you stepped out of your style zone. You may have felt pride in your willingness to do so. Or you may have felt apprehension or fear. Either way, the experience was likely memorable, leaving you with a sense of fulfillment and accomplishment, regardless of the outcome.

Your style zone makes life easier because it gives you a place to comfortably operate from. But, every now and again, try pushing the boundaries of your self-imposed limitations. You may discover a whole new world is waiting for you just outside your natural style.

The Chameleon Student

As Dee and Ivory learned in *A Trip to the Beach*, we tend to stay in our natural style until someone or something pulls us out of it. Attending a new school inevitably causes us to stretch and adapt to new situations. In high school, we have greater control over our schedule than we did in middle school. College takes that freedom to a higher level. We live in dorms, manage our own money and determine the course of our lives. No pressure, right?

Teachers and professors may pull you out of your natural style and comfort zone. Beyond the classroom, you will cultivate new relationships, juggle priorities, collaborate on team projects and work towards goals.

Throughout these endeavors, you need all four styles to be successful. Sometimes, you must don the Eagle hat. Other times, you need to be the Parrot, Dove or Owl. Your least comfortable style provides the greatest opportunity for growth.

Use your school experience to try on new hats. They may feel awkward at first, but the more you wear them, the better they will fit. Stretch yourself, and the hats will stretch with you.

For instance, a Parrot who finds it challenging to manage money could volunteer to be the treasurer of a club. Initially, it may be exhausting to track receipts and balance the checkbook. After some practice, managing money will become more natural, and that new skillset will serve the Parrot later in life.

School is the place to try on new behaviors. Just don't expect to be perfect when you step out of your comfort zone. It may feel uncomfortable at first, but that's where the learning and excitement occurs.

- BREAK YOUR ROUTINE. Do things differently.

- TAKE SMALL STEPS in order to leap out of your comfort zone into something manageable.

- CELEBRATE THE SMALL STEPS you take out of your comfort zone.

- LET GO OF PERFECTIONISM and give yourself permission to fail.

- BE COURAGEOUS. Feel the fear and do it anyway.

The Speech

The Council Tree's mighty limbs stretched in every direction from a massive trunk. Many of its branches were as long as some of the forest's tallest trees, which, on this special day, made it the perfect venue for the big event.

Eagles flew in from all parts of Home and capped the top of the tree. Just below them, the parrots presented a band of blues, reds, yellows, and greens that brightened the forest scenery. The owls arrived early and positioned themselves in the center of the tree directly in front of the stage. Their location afforded them the perfect angle from which to watch the speakers address the crowd. Small groups of doves were scattered throughout the tree in pairs and small groups, filling in the gaps made by the other birds. The entire community gathered for the celebration, except for the squirrels. They seemed to have wandered off.

Simon's white dove feathers blended into the sea of birds that perched around him. He stood on a log to the right of the stage, which gave him easy access to center stage when it was his time.

Everyone had been looking forward to this day . . . well, almost everyone. Simon was gratified to have been the leader of the Pasture Project, which was formed to clean up the swamp and return it to a thriving pasture. After months of work, the project was complete. But this was the day he was dreading. In fact, this day almost stopped him from taking on a leadership role in the first place.

Simon watched the Council President, a short, round owl, explain the details of the project. She described the entire process, complete with charts, statistics, and before-and-after drawings. The speaker took special care to provide a full account of the various challenges they had encountered and how Simon had pulled everyone together to fix them.

Simon stood reluctantly, watching as if he were in a fog. "This is an honor?" he reflected. "I have to stand here in front of everyone and talk about what a great job I did? I succeeded in transforming the swamp and this . . . *this* is my reward. It feels more like a punishment." He sighed in resignation of his fate.

Two parrots watched from a perch high in the Council Tree. They spoke with each other throughout the president's talk. "Simon is up next," a small, green parrot whispered.

"I know. He's not going to like this," responded a large red parrot. "This is a really big crowd. Doves don't like to speak in front of large groups."

"You got that right! He must be freaking out!" said the green parrot.

"I feel bad for him. He'll never be able to pull this off. They should have asked someone else to deliver the speech for him," added the red parrot.

"That would have been the kinder thing," the green parrot agreed.

The longer the Council President spoke, the more nervous Simon became. The idea of making a speech to a small group was scary enough. But this was a large group. Everybody was here.

For days Simon had obsessed about this moment. What if he doesn't remember what he is supposed to say? What if he forgets to mention someone? What if he offends someone by introducing one volunteer before another volunteer who played a bigger role on the project? As Simon's time approached, so did the butterflies in his stomach. He felt physically ill at the thought of looking out at all those eyes staring back at him. Now, his speech was just moments away. The owl was winding down her talk and beginning to introduce him. "Oh, my gosh," the dove thought. "Here it is. I really have to do this."

The owl continued. "And so it is both my honor and privilege to introduce to you the individual who made this all possible. Without his hard work and dedication, we would not be here today. Without further ado, I would like you to give a warm Home welcome to our guest of honor, Simon."

"Here we go," said the red parrot.

"I can't watch," replied the green parrot as he partially covered his eyes with his wing.

The group welcomed Simon with rousing applause and cheers, especially the parrots, who sounded louder than anyone else. Simon took a long . . . slow . . . deep breath and walked deliberately to the podium. The parrots continued to cheer.

"I can do this," Simon told himself.

"Thank you," the dove said, as he gestured for the group to settle down.

Simon took his time to scan the audience, as if he were making eye contact with each individual separately. "Today is not about me," he began. "Today is about the selfless effort put forth by so many. I am humbled by the commitment of those who gave so much of themselves for the benefit of all."

"Hey, he's off to a good start," the green parrot observed.

"Yes, he is," the surprised red parrot agreed.

"I'd like to take a moment to share some of the special things that were done to get us where we are today. First, I'd like to tell you about . . ."

Simon spoke for nearly twenty minutes. He pointed out contributions both great and small. He remembered everyone who had done anything to help with the project, and his speech was met with raucous applause.

"Well, I'll be darned," said the red parrot.

"I can't believe it either," added the green parrot. "That was really good! I didn't know he had it in him."

Just then, a small voice radiated from a branch next to the two parrots. Xenia and her young apprentice, Xander, had overheard the parrots' conversation. Xenia looked at them and said, "When you believe that others are only capable of what their personality might predict, you limit what they can do and who they can become."

The parrots looked at each other and winced. By the time they turned to thank the chameleon, she and her young friend were gone.

"I guess we underestimated Simon's ability," the red parrot acknowledged.

"The chameleon did raise a good point. Just because he's a dove doesn't mean that he can't talk effectively in front of a large group. I suppose we can do anything we want to if we put our minds to it—even if it's something uncomfortable," said the green parrot.

The parrot pals looked at each other, feeling a bit guilty that they had ever doubted Simon.

As the event came to an end, the two parrots approached Simon to congratulate him, both on the work he had done in beautifying the pasture and on his wonderful speech. But when they reached the dove, he looked exhausted. This surprised the parrots, as they were usually brimming with energy after being in the spotlight.

While the parrots told Simon he had done a great job, the dove downplayed his role and gave all the credit to the rest of his team. This, too, surprised the parrots, but they dismissed it quickly and invited Simon to join them at an after-party.

"Thank you so much," Simon replied, "but I really need to get home and recover from all this."

The parrots wondered why Simon needed to recover, but as they flew off to their post-meeting celebration, they recalled what Xenia had taught them.

Chameleon Wisdom

*If we treat people as they ought
to be, we help them become what
they are capable of becoming.*
—JOHANN WOLFGANG VON GOETHE

While we tend to anticipate specific strengths and weaknesses in others based on their natural style, we can all benefit by learning behaviors that are not typically associated with our primary style. These learned behaviors can be just as strong as our innate ones. When we only consider natural strengths and discount learned behaviors, we stifle the development of new skills. Furthermore, when we hold limiting beliefs about what others are capable of achieving, we restrict their potential.

When the red-and-green parrots in *The Speech* were discussing Simon's probability of success, they did not believe that he was capable of talking in front of so many onlookers. They assumed that public speaking skills did not reside in the domain of a dove. Fortunately for Simon, they kept their comments to themselves. If Simon had learned about their lack of confidence in him, he could have lost some of his own confidence.

Consider what would have happened if one of those parrots was Simon's manager in the workplace. It is unlikely he would have been given the opportunity to make that speech. The parrots would have deprived him of the chance to develop new skills, build confidence, and expand the boundaries of his style zone.

When we believe that others are not capable of expanding their style zone, we do not offer them opportunities to stretch themselves beyond their style zone. This lack of opportunity holds them down—limits them to where they are. Ironically, the intentions of those who hold limiting beliefs may not be negative. In fact, they may very well be perceived to be compassionate.

An owl might try to protect someone from providing poor quality work. A dove or parrot might not wish to make someone feel socially uncomfortable. And an eagle might not want to put someone in a position that limits results. In the end, however, the intention does not matter because the impact is the same: high expectations lead to opportunity and high performance, while low expectations lead to limitations and poor results.

While there is little doubt that our short-term success is driven by our strengths, our long-term development is based on our ability to transcend our existing skills. Growth comes when we extend beyond the edges of our past experiences.

Consider an office owl who is not given the opportunity to make a big presentation to a high-profile client. Making the presentation could make the owl temporarily uncomfortable, but taking on the challenge will enable her to grow and expand her capacity. So the next time a similar opportunity arises, she would not feel as anxious. New, learned behaviors may never create excitement, but the negative, draining effects can be minimized with practice . . . if given the opportunity.

Consider a parrot whose owl spouse takes care of all of their financial matters. The owl does not trust the parrot to track things properly, so she never teaches him how to manage their money.

And why would she trust him? From her perspective, managing finances is not a natural parrot skill. When the owl unexpectedly passes away, the parrot has no idea what do and is left without any financial skills. While the parrot may not have enjoyed dealing with the checkbook and the bills (and possibly despised every minute of it), he surely could have learned how to do it. His owl wife failed to activate his potential because she thought it was outside of his style zone.

Visualize an eagle with a group of his close college friends. Whenever someone needs advice about how to handle a crisis, they immediately call upon him to swoop in and save the day. But when an upset friend needs comforting or an empathetic ear, they never ask the eagle to help. When the eagle marries, his spouse is constantly disappointed by his lack of support and validation. No surprise there, since the skill of being emotionally available during difficult times had never been developed by him. The eagle's college friends had never given him the chance to try new behaviors. If they had, they might have been surprised.

Picture a young dove child whose father declined to place him in the awkward position of approaching his teacher about a problem with a grade. To protect his son, the dove parent made the call himself. And why shouldn't he? When he was young, he hated it when his mother made him do things that made him feel uncomfortable. He had vowed long ago that he would never do that to his own child. But now, his son lacks the confidence to stand in his own power and find his own voice.

We communicate expectations to the people around us in conscious ways through our words and in unconscious ways through our tone and body language. A smile to a child walking to the plate in their first little league game builds their confidence. Likewise, the wince you make when you ask someone if he or she is comfortable trying something new conveys volumes.

All of us stay in our comfortable style zones until the world nudges us out of them. When you set high expectations that stretch people out of their zones, they will rise to meet those challenges. When you believe in someone more than they believe in themselves, you build their confidence and increase their potential. You also strengthen your relationship with them.

When you set low expectations for others, they are likely to do only as much as you think they can, especially if you are in a leadership position (manager, coach, parent, or teacher). When we limit others, we limit our relationship with them.

Give others the chance to step out of their style zones, and be there to support them when they do. Recognize their discomfort and honor their courage. Be supportive and accept that the quality or the results may not be perfect the first time through . . . but that is how we learn. Provide positive recognition for their effort, and know that you have helped others to be the best they can be.

The Chameleon Student

Our schoolyears provide us with opportunities to take on leadership roles. Leading a club or a team gives us the power to stretch people beyond their comfort zones while supporting their growth. These challenges can instill confidence that will benefit others throughout their lives.

When people work in an unfamiliar style, they may seem flustered and uncertain. Resist the temptation to immediately bail them out at the first sign of trouble. A person's personality style does not limit their potential, but rescuing someone from discomfort does.

Sometimes people don't seem to fit in with the rest of their group. Consider a team of engineering majors comprised of all Owls and one outlier Parrot. One might assume incorrectly that this Parrot will struggle in a technical, analytical major because her style is different from everyone else's. Their perceptions could limit the Parrot's self-esteem and potential. But just because people are different, doesn't mean they can't succeed. They will succeed in a different way.

When you meet people whose styles don't seem to match their roles, take notice. These individuals may help you reject assumptions and see challenges in a new and creative light. Great leaders know how to integrate unusual skillsets and divergent viewpoints into their teams.

As a leader, you are responsible for how the group works together and the results it achieves. If you believe that people are limited by their personality, you limit their potential. Embody the flexible traits of a Chameleon leader and you will enable people to go far beyond their current role.

For example, leaders tend to delegate tasks. Throughout this book, you likely have seen the benefits of matching people with roles that fit their skills, desires and style. They will work with less stress and capitalize on their strengths.

On the other hand, people have a chance to stretch and grow when they work out of the familiar comfort zone of their style. If you delegate work to someone whose style doesn't align with the role, support that person every step of the way.

Using *The Speech* fable as an analogy, consider a Dove who must present in front of a large group. He feels uncomfortable and nervous. Instead of merely delegating the task and wishing him well, practice the speech together. Give the Dove positive feedback and bolster his self-esteem.

Remember, you are more than just your style, and so are the people around you. Let go of assumptions and open up to the possibilities.

- ENCOURAGE POSITIVE THINKING in others.

- EMBRACE FAILURE as a learning opportunity.

- BELIEVE IN OTHERS and they will believe in themselves.

- SET THE BAR HIGH. Expectations can affect reality and create self-fulfilling prophecies.

The Lost Bird
Department

This was the day Ivory had been looking forward to. The clear blue sky set the stage for the world of possibilities that awaited her. She was about to start a new phase of her life. She was beginning her first job as a contributing member of Home.

This year the Lost Bird Department was in desperate need of assistance, and numerous recruits had committed to help. Many of the tasks assigned to the birds in this department had been arranged long ago. Dee, for example, like the eagles before her, was destined to become a scout. Dee would spend her days scouring the skies above the forest. Her keen eyesight would help her locate lost birds who entered the airspace above Home. While Dee worked as an apprentice to an experienced scout, she would gain the skills necessary to identify flight patterns typical of lost birds. Dee stretched her wings in preparation for her big day.

As a young dove, Simon knew he would be a host for the Lost Bird Department. He was perfectly suited to nurture lost birds with words of support and to provide them with food and a nice tree to sleep in. Simon prepared for his new job by gathering snacks for those in need.

While Ivory was excited to play her part in supporting the community, the role she would take was a mystery to all. After her parrot parents had died suddenly during the Spinning Wind a decade ago, Carl's parents took her in and raised her as their own. Day after day, she watched her new owl family return from work and discuss everything that happened during their day. As mappers, Carl's parents created detailed maps that guided lost birds on their way. They regularly talked about how their work was making a difference. They loved their jobs.

Before they passed away, Ivory's parents were prominent greeters for the Department. When a scout located a lost bird, the hapless fellow was brought directly to a greeter. It was the greeter's responsibility to give the newcomers a tour of Home and make them feel welcome until a host had gathered suitable food for them and located a place for them to rest. Ivory liked the idea of becoming a greeter and thought she would make an excellent tour guide.

Would Ivory follow in the footsteps of her parrot parents and become a greeter, or would she take on the mapper role of her adopted owl parents? Maybe she would surprise everyone and choose to become a scout or a host. Nobody wanted to pressure her. The selection of a job was a personal choice, and the owls wanted her to decide for herself.

For weeks Ivory wrestled with the decision. She recalled her days as a young parrot, listening to her parents share stories about the interesting cast of characters they met as greeters. She also spent the past ten years listening to the owls clearly describe their jobs as mappers. She hoped she could be as inspired by her work as they were with theirs.

The day had come for Ivory to declare her choice. She arrived at the Lost Bird Department ready to announce her decision. In honor of the owls who had taken her in, she selected the role of mapper. She had taken Map Making 101 in Flight School and had done pretty well. It wasn't one of her favorite classes because she found the detailed work to be a bit tiring, but she told herself that training for a job was probably much different than performing the job on a daily basis. Practicing in school to make maps didn't feel rewarding, but maybe that was because she wasn't helping anyone during her practice. She was just trying to get good grades.

After sharing her decision with the Bird Resources Director, Ivory was assigned to shadow Clark, the greatest mapper of his generation. Her first day was exhausting, but she attributed that to having to learn all the steps she would have to follow in her new role. The next day drained her as well . . . as did the next day and the one after that. Each day, her feathers seemed a bit more ruffled, but she was getting through it.

Over the coming weeks, the work grew harder, not easier. She slowly gained mapmaking skills, and, in fact, became quite proficient at it. But she was not excited to go to work, and she didn't understand why not. Carl's parents loved being mappers.

After several weeks, Clark approached Ivory to tell her that she had learned the key skills of mapping. He said she would improve further over time, but that she was proficient enough now to take on her first charge. Her apprenticeship had come to end.

"Maybe," she hoped, "I'll enjoy my job now that I have the freedom to do it on my own."

A few hours later, Ivory met her first lost bird. For the first time in quite a while, she was eager to be a mapper. She was excited at the prospect of helping someone on their travels.

Ivory retrieved her clipboard with the Lost Bird Tracking Form she used to document the process, just as she was taught. She methodically started at Step 1: "Conduct intake interview to determine starting point and destination."

The parrot understood that the data she gathered in Step 1 was critical for tracking patterns. She recognized that every detail was significant. Once Step 1 was complete, she moved on to Step 2: "Consult the Map Catalog." She proceeded to the Map Room and began to scour diagrams created by previous mappers.

It was tedious work that required intense focus and concentration. Ivory spent the entire day measuring, drawing, calculating, checking, and rechecking. In the end, she was proud of her creation, but she felt drained.

The next morning, Ivory repeated the process she had performed the day before—interview the lost bird, analyze the extensive catalog, create a map, and confirm the plan's accuracy.

Before long, Ivory was dreading going to work.

One day a scout brought Ivory two quiet little birds who, while traveling together, had lost their way. "Ivory, let's talk," the eagle said.

"Sure thing," answered the parrot. "What can I do for ya'?"

"Do you recognize these guys?" the eagle asked.

The two small birds looked at Ivory with big, sad eyes.

"Hey, you were just here two days ago," Ivory said to the pair. "Are you lost again?"

The birds nodded.

"Didn't you follow the directions I gave you?" Ivory probed.

They didn't know how to respond. Evidently, they followed Ivory's directions, but Ivory had sent them off to fly in circles, and they had never left Home.

The small birds handed Ivory the map she had created, and she immediately understood why they had gotten lost. Even though the map wasn't accurate, she was impressed by her drawing.

The eagle called to a nearby host to take the lost pair aside. The imposing eagle looked directly into Ivory's eyes and said, "Look, this is the third time I've found a lost bird who remained lost after you had helped them. It seems as though your maps, your instructions, or both are not clear enough. I didn't want to mention this before because I recognized that you were new to the job, but your work has not been acceptable."

Ivory felt terrible and apologized to the eagle for creating extra work for him.

"Hey, I don't mind the work. It's what I do. I love my job," the eagle replied.

The parrot grimaced.

"Ivory, I'm sensing that you don't like being a mapper. What's going on?"

Ivory exploded with weeks' worth of frustration. "I can't take it!" she declared. "I thought I would love being a mapper. I listened to Carl's parents rave about this job, and I don't get it."

"It sounds like you're the one who is lost," the eagle observed. "Is there another job you think you'd like better?"

"Now that you ask, I've been watching the greeters taking our lost visitors on tours of Home, and it looks as if they are having a blast!" Ivory said. "In that job, I'd get to meet fascinating travelers and show off our awesome forest. And the best part is, I wouldn't have to draw any maps!"

They both laughed.

"My father once told me," the eagle said, "that if I find a job based on my strengths, my spirit will soar."

"I wish I was doing that," Ivory sighed. "I'm experiencing the opposite. I'm not using my strengths, and my job feels like drudgery."

"Your job should feed your spirit, not drain it," the eagle explained. "What you are experiencing is not good for you or anyone else."

"Especially these little lost fellows," the parrot acknowledged. "It's time for me to stop making maps and start making conversations as a greeter."

"I think everyone would appreciate that," the eagle agreed with a smile.

"I think you're right," Ivory responded. "Now where did those little guys go? One more map couldn't hurt anyone."

The eagle looked at Ivory in disbelief until he noticed the teasing smirk on her face. "Oh, I think it could," the eagle laughed. "How about we leave the maps to those who enjoy making them?"

Chameleon Wisdom

The only way to do great work is to love what you do.
—STEVE JOBS

During our careers we spend about a third of our waking lives at work. One would hope that those hours are being spent doing something that feeds our spirit.

Unfortunately, for most people work is just that . . . *work*. Sometimes it is the environment that does not resonate with us. Other times it is the job itself. There are many variables that impact job satisfaction, but one thing is clear—if our style matches the job and the organization's culture, the work will feed us. If not, it will drain us.

Each style has different career needs. *Eagles*, for example, prefer to work in an environment that allows them to spread their wings and operate freely. They don't like routine work. They prefer a wide range of responsibilities. Eagles favor an environment that values candor and offers opportunity for advancement based on performance.

Like eagles, *parrots* get frustrated when they feel constrained. They need a high degree of interaction with others and thrive when they can socialize and connect with people. They prefer to work for a motivating and empowering manager who provides positive feedback and the freedom to express ideas.

Doves seek a calm and stable work environment that has predictable routines and defined standards. They prefer incremental, rather than revolutionary, change. Doves like to work in a small, tight-knit group that enjoys minimal conflict and a high degree of trust and respect. They value sincere appreciation for a job well done.

Owls like to work within clearly defined expectations and procedures. Because they focus on details, they prefer a private workspace with little interruption. Owls value a business-like environment that offers opportunities to demonstrate their expertise, and they require sufficient time to ensure that they can produce quality results.

In *The Lost Bird Department*, Ivory was in a job that did not match her style. Playing the role of mapper drained her energy. She tried to make it work, but there was no way for her to create long-term success at a job that did not resonate with her social parrot style. Ultimately, she was destined to become a mediocre mapper because her true talents were being underutilized. When she changes her role to greeter, her gifts will be employed, she will become successful, and she will feel fulfilled.

Imagine a young parrot personality whose persuasiveness and verbal adeptness have inspired many people to encourage her to become a lawyer. As she grows older, she internalizes the idea that she would enjoy being an attorney, so off she goes to law school. However, once she begins working as a practicing attorney, she discovers that being is lawyer is far from the dramatic television images she has seen of legal battles in courtrooms. She discovers the job entails more research and writing than she had ever conceived.

This doesn't mean that a parrot cannot be a talented attorney or enjoy being an attorney. But this parrot's personality style did not match what was required of her at work.

Not liking parts of your job description does not necessarily mean you should be dusting off your resume and looking for a new job. Everyone has responsibilities they find distasteful. The question is this: How much of your energy is being zapped by a job or work environment that does not match your style?

If the energy drain is small, look for ways to minimize its impact. Perhaps you can find a coworker with whom you can trade unwanted tasks. Maybe you can talk with your manager about having unpleasant responsibilities removed from your plate.

Take an energy audit of your job. Does the organization's culture feel like a good fit or does it feel out of sync with who you are? Does your job nourish your soul or eat away at your spirit?

Remember, your job should feed you, not drain you.

The Chameleon Student

Growing up, we looked to our parents for guidance. With the best intentions, they steered us in a direction they believed would bring happiness and prosperity.

In many cases, however, parents unwittingly impose their unfulfilled dreams or their family's traditional career upon their children. The mother who was a successful dancer is likely to sign her daughter up for dance classes. Likewise, the father who wasn't allowed to play guitar as a child may buy his son a shiny new six-string for his birthday. Maybe the parents come from a long line of lawyers and expect their child to follow that path.

"You would make a great engineer just like your father and grandfather," says one mother to her son. "You should be a lawyer," a father tells his young daughter.

It is tempting to buy into your parents' story because it's grounding and provides direction. And who wants to disappoint their mother and father? As you mature though, your desires emerge and you get to choose a career. If your path resonates with your style, it will feel easy and natural. If it doesn't, each day will be exhausting.

As the birds learned in *The Lost Bird Department*, do what feeds you. You've probably heard the well-worn advice given to every young adult: Find a job that you love. If it were that easy, would have their dream job, but most do not. Too many people watch the clock, looking forward to the moment they can go home. Just listen to what radio DJs and daily podcasters say. On Monday, they lament that the work week has started again. By Wednesday, they reassure people that the week is halfway over. When Friday finally arrives, they celebrate that they have survived another week and have two days for fun and excitement. Then, the cycle begins all over again on Monday. Sadly, that resonates with most listeners.

How did so many people become miserable at their jobs? The answer goes back to their school years. Have you ever had a teacher who was so bad, that one course ruined a whole subject for you? Maybe you had a class that was so boring, confusing or seemingly pointless that you decided to avoid a career in that field? In college, perhaps you've had an internship filled with menial tasks that didn't resonate with your personality?

Far too many students link their teacher's personality style or their classroom experience with what a job in that field would be like. Imagine an Owl chemistry professor who is obsessed with formulas and memorizing the periodic table. A Parrot student may dislike a class or a professor and assume that a career in chemistry would be dissatisfying.

Consider an Eagle who volunteers in a hospital to see if she would like to become a nurse. She soon becomes disillusioned with nursing because it doesn't seem fast-paced and exciting enough for her. However, she may have had a satisfying career as a nurse in an emergency room, where crises and quick decisions energize her.

Select a major and, ultimately, a career that feeds you. But don't despair if the preparation for that career doesn't excite you. The training and education required for a role is often different from the actual job itself.

Focus on what will ultimately fulfill you in the future, not the teacher, the classwork or the effort it take on that job. It may seem daunting to suffer through the education, but in the long run, the payoff will be worth it. One day, you will turn on the radio, podcast (or whatever exists 10 years from now) on a rainy Monday morning. While the DJ complains about the start of another week, you will feel excited to be back in your element.

- SPEND TIME WITH OTHERS who love their jobs. Let their joy inspire you to re-imagine your career.

- DON'T SETTLE FOR TASKS that drain you. Ask for what you want.

- MAKE SURE THAT EVERY DAY has an element in it of what you love to do.

- CREATE OPPORTUNITIES to engage your hardwiring.

- DO SOMETHING THAT FEEDS YOU. Choose to do what you love.

The Forbidden Swamp

Acheerful sun warmed a summer breeze as it wafted through the air. It was the perfect day to take a meditative stroll through the outer reaches of Home. Xenia enjoyed her alone time. She had discovered the perfect place to connect with the spirit of the forest. Not many creatures ventured this far west of the Great Lake. Her secret spot afforded her the opportunity to sink deeply into the silence of the woods.

The chameleon took pleasure in her oneness with the land. As she walked, she matched her color to the teals, violets, golds, and reds of the flowers nearby. Xenia ambled by a small stream and approached a pungent marshy area. Vines hung above the soggy land, and trees grew out of the water. Cattails and water lilies decorated the landscape, and mosquitoes and dragonflies filled the air.

As she approached the dreaded Forbidden Swamp, she was surprised to hear two voices in the distance. Because of the many spooky stories that had circulated about the dangers of the swamp, it was rarely frequented by the birds or any other forest creatures. Some said that the swamp emitted a powerful gas that could drive you instantly mad. Others said it had the power to change your form into one of a horrible being. Everyone in the forest seemed to know someone who knew someone who had never been heard from again after inhaling the swamp's powerful vapors.

Xenia walked peacefully towards the swamp as if she were impervious to its effects. As she drew closer to the voices, she could see the shadows of an eagle and dove. When she got even closer, she saw they belonged to Dee and Simon.

Though she couldn't make out their words just yet, the tone of their voices indicated that they both seemed troubled. Once Xenia got within earshot, she discovered that Dee was troubled that the other birds thought she was bossy and overbearing, and Simon was upset that they viewed him as passive and weak.

Xenia continued to approach the pair as they continued to express their concerns. Simon felt that if he were female, the others would feel differently about him. "I don't understand why the others view the female doves as friendly and considerate, yet I'm considered a pushover."

Dee echoed Simon's sentiment. She believed that if she were male, others would not criticize her as being bossy. She described one dominating and demanding male eagle who was considered to be a great leader. "I don't get it," complained Dee.

"Me neither," replied Simon.

Xenia chose this moment to appear. "Perhaps I can shed some light on the subject."

The two birds jumped, and Xenia smirked. She always relished the reactions to her surprise visits. "I couldn't help but overhear your conversation, and it sounds like you are both bothered by how others see you."

"You got that right," Dee snapped. "It's not fair that others judge me by my gender."

Xenia turned to Simon, "And you feel judged because you're male?"

"I guess I do," the dove responded.

"It might be helpful for you to see how the other half lives," the chameleon shared.

The eagle and dove looked puzzled.

"Allow me to explain. Simon, would you like to experience how others would see you if you were more like an eagle—full of strength, conviction, and power?"

"Sure," he nodded tentatively.

"And Dee, would you like to see what it would be like if others perceived you as if you were a dove—considerate, thoughtful, and kind?"

"That would be nice for a change," Dee said. "But how . . ."

"Then follow me," Xenia said as she walked towards the Forbidden Swamp. When they reached the edge of the mucky water, she instructed them. "I need you to do exactly what I say and nothing more. Do you understand?"

The two birds looked at each other, not certain of what they had gotten themselves into. However, they trusted Xenia and cautiously agreed to the chameleon's conditions.

"Sit beside me and relax," she guided.

The chameleon nestled her small frame onto a large, dry leaf. She crossed her legs and placed her hands upon her knees. The birds tried to follow suit, but they could not quite get their legs in the same position, so they squatted down on the wet ground.

Xenia continued. "I know that the swamp does not smell good, but do not fear. It will not harm you. Let go of all thought and simply be here in this place at this time. I want you to take three long, slow breaths, each time drawing the air deep into your belly."

Sitting silently, the pair focused on their breathing. "Dee, visualize yourself as soft-spoken, helpful, and caring. See yourself exactly as you would like others to perceive you. Simon, visualize yourself as being strong, confident, and in command of every situation. Feel with every aspect of your being what that would be like. Breathe deeply and think of nothing else."

For the next few minutes, the birds focused intently on seeing themselves as they would like to be seen. Gradually, a strange sensation began to wash over them. Xenia noticed that Simon was sitting up a little straighter. His expression became more serious and resolute. Dee, in contrast, softened her features. She seemed content and peaceful.

"It is done," Xenia announced. "Open your eyes. You are not to speak to each other until the sun disappears below the horizon. Return now to your familiar surroundings. At dusk I will meet you on the large boulder in the center of the field beside the Great Lake. Now go. I will see both of you later."

The two looked at each other, pressed their weight into the ground, and took off into the sky in opposite directions.

Xenia smiled and thought, "This is becoming an interesting day."

Simon soared over the forest. He flew higher and higher until he was looking down on Home from the bottom of the clouds. As he drifted over the forest, he spied two doves, one gray and one white.

The gray dove was crying. Simon landed firmly next to the pair and barked, "What's wrong?"

The gray dove was too shaken to answer, so her friend replied. "She lost a heart-shaped gem that her grandmother gave her. She's afraid it is gone forever."

"That's it?" Simon replied.

"Well, yeah," the white dove said. "It means a lot to her."

"There are lots of heart-shaped gems in the Crystal Cave," Simon stated. "Just go there and get another one. In fact, I believe a group of parrots are heading there tomorrow. Would you like me to ask them to get one for you?"

Both doves looked at Simon in disbelief. "You don't understand," said the sobbing dove. "That stone has sentimental value and cannot be replaced. You can't just . . ."

Simon interrupted. "I understand. You're grandmother gave it to you. But it's gone. I'm just trying to help you to replace it."

Neither dove knew how to respond to Simon's callousness, so the white dove leaned in and suggested, "Maybe it would be best if I comforted her alone."

"Suit yourself," Simon replied as he flew off to see what else was happening in Home.

Across the forest, Dee was aiming toward the treetops, but they seemed higher than usual. The eagle slowed herself down and decided to fly a little closer to the ground. As she dipped downward, she heard shouts coming from a group of nearby owls. She made her way there and was stunned by what she saw. A newborn groundhog was wedged in a tree hollow, and several owls were debating how to resolve the situation. They had suggested a few options and were now evaluating each one. In the meantime, the groundhog was becoming increasingly agitated. Someone had to do something.

"Thank goodness," one of the owls declared. "Dee is here. She will know what do."

Another owl asked, "Dee, can you help us out? We need to make a decision, and we cannot seem to agree on a course of action. We need someone to make the call."

Dee's gaze was fixed on the groundhog. She uneasily watched him squirm. He looked as if he had an itch on his hind quarters that could not be scratched. She felt his frustration as deeply as if it were happening to her.

"Well, Dee?" another owl pressed.

"So?" inquired yet another.

"Well, I'm not sure," replied the eagle. "Can you hold on for a moment? I'd like to talk with our furry friend. He seems rather upset."

For the next few minutes, Dee chatted supportively with the groundhog. The owls watched in surprise. Dee's words were comforting and helped to calm him.

"Excuse me, Dee," one of the owls interrupted. "We already spoke to the groundhog, determined the cause of his predicament, and discussed his physical condition. He has no injuries. He's just stuck, and we need to get him out of there."

"I'm not sure what to do," Dee said. "But he seems a lot more relaxed now."

"Dee," one of the owls cracked. "If you are not going to help, you are just in the way."

Dee shrugged and decided that she was distracting the owls from making a decision. She wished the groundhog well and offered a few more supportive words to the owls before she left them to sift through their options and determine a course of action.

The setting sun began to creep toward the horizon as Dee and Simon headed to the designated meeting place. Simon arrived first and Dee shortly thereafter.

Xenia had blended so flawlessly into the rock she was on that only the bright yellow glow of her eyes was visible. Beside her, a set of smaller orbs appeared. They belonged to her protégé, Xander. Xenia introduced the young chameleon to the birds, who were beginning to feel more like themselves again.

Dee spoke first. "What did you do to us?"

Xenia smiled. "Oh, don't worry about that. Tell me about your day."

"Before I tell you what happened, you've got to tell me what you did," the eagle insisted.

"I did not do anything," Xenia answered. "The swamp emits an invisible gas that magnifies your thoughts. The effects are only temporary, but they can be intense."

"Intense? That's one way to describe it," Dee snarled.

"So how was your day?" the chameleon asked again.

"How was my day?" Dee replied. "Well, let's see. I discovered that trees are really tall and the forest can be dangerous. I came across a groundhog who got stuck in a tree hollow, and the owls had no idea how to help him."

"Did you help them?" Xenia asked.

Dee hesitated before saying, "Not exactly."

Dee explained that she wasn't quite herself and that her initial impulse was to ease the groundhog's stress. The owls, on the other hand, just wanted her to make a decision.

"Did you tell them what to do?" the chameleon probed.

"Not exactly," the eagle repeated. "I didn't feel comfortable telling them what to do. I just wanted to ease the groundhog's distress."

Xenia squinted her eyes and said, "Fascinating."

Dee replied, "As I said, I wasn't exactly myself."

"It appears that being someone else is not as great as it may seem," the chameleon said.

Dee nodded in agreement.

Xenia then turned her gaze to the dove. "And you, Simon, tell me about your day."

Simon looked away when he admitted, "I'm a little ashamed."

"Why is that?"

"I came across a dove who was very upset. I tried to fix the problem, but instead I should have consoled her. I did not act very nice."

Xenia stood up straight, looked intently into Simon's eyes, and said, "It appears that the same behavior can be perceived differently depending upon your gender."

"But that's not fair," Dee asserted angrily. "I should be allowed to do what male eagles do without being called bossy."

"Indeed," Xenia confirmed. "I guess you have an important decision to make. What matters more to you, how you see yourself or how others see you?"

Simon reflected, "You're saying that male doves can act the same as female doves, but that those actions may not be interpreted the same way."

"Precisely!" Xenia exclaimed. "Simon, I know you do not want those around you to see you as weak. However, your peers do not see you as weak. They see you as a compassionate friend. And Dee, you do not want to be thought of as bossy. While sometimes you may be viewed as being bossy, your peers also view you as a confident leader. You each have wonderful traits that you can be proud of."

Dee and Simon were beginning to feel a lot better about themselves.

The chameleon took a moment to allow her words to resonate and then said, "Your personality is your own. Do not let others define it for you. You were gifted with a specific set of strengths, but those strengths come with a related set of weaknesses. If you trade away your gifts for a new set you consider to be better, you will lose the essence of what makes you special. And, you would not only be acquiring new strengths, you would also be gaining a whole new set of challenges."

Xenia's granite gray color transformed into a rich crimson that matched the evening sky. Xander followed his teacher's lead and shifted his color. Just before the two chameleons departed, Xenia asked her student to share what he had learned. He cleared his throat and said, "Accept yourself fully and you will be free of the need to be accepted by others."

Dee and Simon could see that Xenia was beaming with pride at her student's response. The teacher looked back, gave the birds a wink, and faded into the sunset. The eagle and dove watched as the sky turned a deeper shade of red. Simon said, "I kinda like who you are, Dee. You don't need to act like a dove."

Dee responded, "Yeah. I like who you are, too. Besides, there's only room for one eagle."

They both laughed and, together, enjoyed the spectacle of the setting sun.

Chameleon Wisdom

To be successful, you don't have to change who you are. You have to become more of who you are.
—SALLY HOGSHEAD

While gender roles have certainly changed over the past fifty years, gender stereotypes still exist. These labels impact both men and women. They can inhibit well-being and limit a person's full potential. As we unconsciously conform to cultural views of femininity and masculinity, we may be ignoring our innate personality style.

The notion that all men display more eagle characteristics—being direct, daring, and risk-taking—and women more dove-like qualities—soft-spoken, sensitive, and good listeners—is not grounded in reality. Of course we know that men can be good listeners and women can be assertive. Female eagles are just as confident and candid as their male counterparts, and male doves are just as empathetic and compassionate as female doves.

But due to cultural norms, we may perceive the same action differently, depending upon which gender displays it. In *The Forbidden Swamp*, Simon and Dee felt as if they would have been treated differently if they were the opposite gender. The eagle felt as if her behaviors would have been more socially acceptable if she were male. The dove felt as if his actions would have been more acceptable if he were female. As such, they sought to change their style to conform to societal expectations. In so doing, they discovered that changing who they were resulted in detrimental consequences. By giving up their strengths, they lost the essence of their true nature.

Whether we seek to change ourselves because of societal pressure, cultural expectations, or any other reason, understand that every strength is paired with a corresponding weakness. While our strengths and weaknesses may seem contradictory, they are actually interdependent. One cannot exist without the other. And when we exchange one strength for a new strength, we also pick up its related weakness.

Consider how each style listens to others. *Eagles* are bottom-line listeners. They do not want to be bothered with minute details or long explanations. If you do not get to the point quickly, eagles will either cut you off or tune you out. *Parrots* are responsive listeners who like to share personal stories about topics at hand. Like the eagles, they do not tune into details. *Doves* are empathetic listeners who pick up on the emotion of others as they tune into tone and body language. *Owls* are analytical listeners who focus on facts and logic. They compare what is said by others to what they know or think should be said. If there is a match, the owls have no problem. However, if the information received does not coincide with their previously held knowledge, the owls will ask a lot of questions.

What would happen if someone tried to change his listening style? Imagine a parrot salesperson who is going on sales calls and bringing high energy and passion to his prospects. He spends little time describing his product, but his excitement is so contagious, the finer points of what he is selling do not seem to matter.

At home his wife often tells him that he is not a good listener. She cites his inability to pay attention to details and complains that when he is speaking, he talks excessively about himself. After years of hearing he is a poor listener, he begins to think his wife may be correct, and he internalizes the notion that this behavior may be impacting his effectiveness at work. As a result, he decides it is time to become a better listener and communicator in every aspect of his life.

Now, when he heads out on sales calls, he focuses on providing details about the features and benefits of his products. He asks many questions and tries to listen without interrupting to share personal anecdotes. While this new approach takes a tremendous amount of energy to sustain, he acknowledges he has become a more attentive and analytical listener. At home, his wife is ecstatic. But at work, he is surprised to see that his sales have gone down . . . not up.

While the parrot salesman gave up talking about himself, which his wife had considered a weakness, he picked up a new weakness—not connecting with his sales prospects. He traded his stories and enthusiasm for attention to the details. As he did so, he lost the essence of what made him successful.

Pressure to conform to the world around us comes from many places. Society imposes unstated expectations on us. Organizational cultures encourage us to fit in if we want to be successful. Even parents and spouses place pressure on us to act how *they* think we should act. But in the end, we are not good for others if we are not good for ourselves.

Don't trade away your true self just to fit in. If you do, be aware that you will pick up a whole new set of weaknesses, and you will never feel like you are who you were meant to be. Developing new skills is a good thing, but do not give up what makes you special.

The Chameleon Student

Two themes are at play in *The Forbidden Swamp*. The first relates to gender and our perceptions of assertive, female Eagles and soft-spoken, male Doves. The second is the desire to be someone who we are not.

Let's start with gender stereotypes. In the 1950s, a dominant Eagle woman in the workplace would have raised eyebrows. So too would a Dove man who cried during his child's high school graduation. Attitudes have changed a lot since then, but historical stereotypes about men and women persist. Advertising, television, movies and music frequently reinforce them.

Stereotypes only perpetuate if we pass them down. Beliefs about gender roles form over generations, but we have the power to change them. We can choose to value the assertive woman and the sensitive man. We can appreciate people, male or female, who stand in the power of their convictions or openly express emotion.

Your behaviors can demonstrate acceptance and appreciation. For example, if you're in charge of assigning roles on a team, prioritize style over gender. Challenge yourself to see people's skills, strengths and personality without the lens of traditional gender stereotypes.

That brings us to the second point: If we try to be someone we are not, perhaps to fulfill a gender stereotype, we forsake our natural strengths. When we trade away our style for a new one, we pick up both the strengths and weaknesses of that other style. An Owl student who feels that schoolwork takes too long to complete can tap into Eagle energy and work faster. She may complete her work with time to spare, but she'll make more mistakes.

When you admire fellow students for their abilities, recognize that they may admire abilities that come easily and naturally for you. Develop new skills, but do not try to become a different person. You are okay just the way you are.

Find a social group and a career that resonates with you and you won't need to change a thing. You will be celebrated for being you.

- BE INDEPENDENT OF THE FEELINGS OF OTHERS. Be yourself . . . everyone else is already taken.

- WORK ON AREAS that you would like to improve, but don't try to be someone else.

- THE BEST WAY TO SHOW LOVE is to accept others, not try to improve them.

- DON'T CHANGE FOR OTHERS. If people do not like you for who you are, decide if they are people you want in your life.

- DON'T TRY TO CHANGE OTHERS to satisfy your needs. They will ultimately resent it.

The Summer Festival

With the last remnants of summer fading away, the residents of Home were preparing for the cooler days of fall. From the smallest dove to the largest eagle, the forest dwellers were eager to spread their wings and breathe in the sun's warmth one last time.

The last weekend of summer was a time to honor everything the season had bestowed upon them. And for as long as anyone could remember, the community bid goodbye to this special time of year with a festival. Since summer embodied light, heat, freedom, and joy, the Summer Festival had to capture that sense of playfulness.

Each year, one owl and one parrot were selected to coordinate, plan, and run the festivities. Carl and Ivory were chosen to lead this year's event.

Carl prepared to apply the owl wisdom his mother, Crystal, had passed down to him when she advised, "Aim twice, strike once." He was tasked with supervising food and logistics and was looking forward to organizing an efficiently managed event.

Ivory's red, yellow, and green parrot feathers symbolized the energy she planned to infuse into this year's festivities—or "The

Ultimate Extravaganza," as she liked to call it. She was in charge of the activities and entertainment.

With just two days to go before the celebration took place, Carl reviewed the scrolls containing his detailed plans, charts, and timelines. He arranged the food for the different species, taking all dietary restrictions into consideration. He designed an overall map of the grounds and established a system for the doves to watch over their increasing number of little ones. He even prepared a rain plan in case of inclement weather.

Ivory selected a few of her favorite games and made up a couple new ones. She even procured a few Venus flytraps for an activity that she named "Snapper." The last time she ran an activity using these plants, it didn't go so well, but the parrot was certain she worked out the kinks. This time it was going to be hilarious, or so she hoped. "What's the worst thing that could happen?" she wondered.

The big day arrived. As the sun's first rays began to sweep across Home, the two leaders met in the Great Field that bordered the Great Lake. When Carl arrived, he saw Ivory circling speedily above the water, rising and lowering as she went. He had never seen a parrot fly so fast.

"Oh, just wonderful," the owl thought sarcastically. "We've got work to do, and Ivory is already playing games."

Carl hopped onto a branch that hung over the water and called to his partner. "If it is not too much trouble, can you come over here so we can get started? We have much to do."

"Sure thing," Ivory bellowed as she made one more quick lap around the field.

Carl had barely glanced up from his scrolls before Ivory landed with a thump beside him. The owl immediately began dictating instructions. "I have prioritized our morning and would like to start by establishing a perimeter to contain the day's events. After that, I will prepare the day care area for the young ones. Once that is complete, I will . . ."

The list went on and on. Although Ivory didn't hear much of what he was saying, she let him talk. When Carl was done, the parrot asked, "Since you seem to have everything under control, how about I go set up the games?"

"That is acceptable," Carl replied. "When you are done, please return to me so we can determine what needs to happen next."

"Will do," Ivory said, as she flitted off for the area that Carl designated as "Games" on one of the tracking scrolls he had created.

Carl was happy to be left alone so he could focus on his work. Before long, the sun would be overhead and everyone would be arriving. Carl felt burdened by how much was still left to do.

By the time Ivory made her way back to Carl, the owl hadn't even left to perform his first project. He was still reviewing his tasks on paper to ensure everything was in the proper order and that no critical steps were missed.

Ivory could immediately see the concern on Carl's face, and she wanted to help. "The games are ready," Ivory announced. "Gimme something. Anything at all. Whadya got for me?"

Carl frowned because he worried that Ivory would not follow the plan exactly and that her actions would thrust the entire event into disarray. But he needed the help, so he hesitantly said, "I suppose you can set up the food for the eagles. It is right over there. Now, listen carefully. When you place the food down, there are a few things I would like to review with you. First, as you . . .”

"Don't worry, I've got it," Ivory exclaimed.

She zigged and zagged her way toward the spot marked, "Eagle—Food." Carl returned to his scrolls. Everything looked in order.

A few minutes later, the parrot returned to Carl, proud to have fulfilled her assignment. "Now what?" she asked eagerly.

"You are finished?" asked Carl.

"Yup. That wasn't hard. What's next?"

"How is that possible?" he thought. His desire to get everything accomplished overwhelmed his need to question her thoroughness. So he gave her the next assignment and continued his work.

Carl tried to focus, but all he could do was speculate on how Ivory had set up the eagle's food. There was, after all, a very specific way he wanted the food arranged. His concerns about Ivory not following his guidelines gnawed at him until he couldn't take it anymore. He had to see what she had done.

Carl marched quickly across the field to the eagle's food area and gasped. "What the . . . ? This is not right," he protested. "I provided her with a clear diagram of how the eagles prefer their food to be arranged, or at least how they *should* want their food to be arranged, and this is not even close. I suppose if I want something done right, I have to do it myself."

As Carl reorganized just about everything Ivory had prepared, he berated himself for his carelessness. "I should have known better. That parrot is just getting in the way."

A few minutes later, Ivory flew by the eagle's food. Her smile turned to a confused pout. "Wait a minute. What happened here? Did someone rearrange this?"

And then it struck her. "Carl did this! He didn't like the way I set the food out, so he took it upon himself to redo it! Why did he ask me to do it in the first place if he was going to rearrange it? Well, I'll be darned if I'm going to waste any more of my time doing things that are going to be redone."

Ten minutes passed before Carl realized that Ivory was nowhere to be found. He scanned the sky above the Great Field and couldn't find her. He looked above the Great Lake, but she wasn't there either. When he looked over the grounds to the western tip of the pasture, he spotted her. "What on earth is she doing?"

The owl shook off his stunned disbelief and charged toward Ivory. With each step, he got angrier. When he got about ten feet away from her, he launched into a tirade. "Why are you playing with the Venus flytraps? Don't you know how much we have to do? We were selected for this job, and we are tasked with doing it right. This festival is not going to set itself up!"

Ivory shrugged, "That may be true, but it doesn't get *reset* by itself, either."

Carl didn't know what to say. He wanted to point out that he wouldn't have changed her food arrangement if she had done it right the first time, but he knew that would not help the situation. He just sighed in frustration.

Ivory then added, "How about you organize things how you want them, and I'll just stay out of your way. I'd rather get snapped at by a Venus flytrap than get poked by your lack of confidence."

Carl felt conflicted. While it was true he did not trust the parrot, it was only because she displayed disregard for the process. Carl never intended to hurt Ivory's feelings, but he could see he had done just that. As they walked across the Great Field together, Carl apologized to Ivory. The parrot reluctantly agreed to set up the welcome area, with one condition.

Carl stopped in his tracks to focus on what Ivory had to say next. The parrot looked directly into his big owl eyes and stated, "If your way is the only way to do something right, you will end up being the only one who is going to do it."

Carl knew that Ivory was right, and he nodded in agreement. The owl considered his words carefully before he replied. "I appreciate your help, and I will try to be open to other ways of doing things."

"That's all I'm asking," the parrot returned as she clapped him on the back a bit too enthusiastically. "Now let's get this extravaganza started!"

Chameleon Wisdom

Everyone driving slower than you is an idiot. Everyone driving faster than you is a maniac.
—GEORGE CARLIN

Have you ever seen two parents in the same household, two managers in the same department, or two people with the same job perform their roles differently while being equally effective? Yet, if you were to ask one of those folks to describe the optimal way to play that role, they would inevitably describe their own approach.

It is not unreasonable to think that our way is the best way. Because our achievements have proved to us that our way works, we hold them as concrete evidence to support our assumption.

We solve problems and live our lives in a way that is consistent with our personality. While style is not a predictor of success, it is a predictor of how we are likely to go about achieving it.

Consider the approach of the four bird styles: *Eagles* drive results by taking bold risks to accomplish big things that have never been done before. *Parrots'* eternal optimism and faith in others drive them to try out new ideas and trust others to help them along the way. *Doves* achieve success by cultivating long-term relationships and creating a supportive and nurturing environment. *Owls* maintain efficient systems to ensure consistency and attain quality results.

In *The Summer Festival*, Carl's owl style compelled him to follow his own high standards of excellence. He had a specific way he wanted things done, and he forced those expectations on Ivory. This served to alienate and discourage his friend. To the owl, the adage "If you want something done right, you have to do it yourself" became "If I want something done *my* way, I have to do it *myself.*"

Like Carl, we each unknowingly impose this perspective on others more than we might think. However, while our perspectives are based on our own experiences, they do not represent the *only* way to achieve objectives.

Whether we are at home, work, or with friends, the "My Way" attitude creates hierarchy and inhibits trust. Since strong relationships are built on a foundation that allows *both* individuals to get their needs met, compromise is sometimes necessary. If one spouse, partner, or coworker is subordinated to following the rules and methods of the other, resentment and animosity can undermine their foundation.

Imagine two parents who have different views on how to deal with a child who has disrespected a friend. The eagle parent simply wants to explain to the child how her behavior has made her friend feel. Afterward, the eagle is willing to drop the issue entirely. The dove parent wants the child to call her friend and apologize so they can get back on good terms. Both parents think their way is the right way to handle the situation, and each is closed to the other's approach. When they entrench themselves in their own perspectives, they invalidate their partner's solution, and they also invalidate who their partner is as an individual.

Parents who hyper-control every aspect of a child's life are referred to as "helicopter parents." These mothers and fathers swoop in and hover over everything their children do. While they believe they are being helpful, they are actually decreasing their children's confidence and increasing their anxiety. Hovering parents send messages to their children that they are not capable of figuring things out for themselves. This, in turn, creates a self-fulfilling prophecy—the children stop trying to identify solutions to their own problems and become even more dependent. This cycle then boomerangs back to reinforce the parents' notion that they need to be more involved.

Imagine an owl/dove child who enjoys spending time with his one and only friend. The two companions are inseparable. The mother, a parrot, is dismayed that her child is not part of a larger social group. She is constantly telling her child that he should try to make additional friends. The more the child resists, the harder the mother pushes. The mother is inadvertently conveying to her child that his approach to friendship is wrong. By imposing her style on her child, the mother is sending a message to him that he is inadequate.

While the mother is trying to be helpful, she is actually being harmful. Her actions are driven by her own experience that happiness is derived by having many friends. She incorrectly assumes that if having many friends makes her happy, it will also make her son happy. Unfortunately for her offspring, the mother's actions have the inverse effect of decreasing her child's self-esteem.

At work, managers who have a "My Way" attitude are referred to as micromanagers. Like helicopter parents, they impose their methodology and, in turn, their style on others. Imagine an eagle who has been successful in his role for many years. He gets a new owl-like manager and, suddenly, it seems as if he cannot do anything right. His manager is critical of the processes he uses. The eagle's quality seems to be constantly under fire. He feels like his initiative and creativity are being stifled by a boss who criticizes everything he does.

Over time, the manager starts taking over some of the eagle's responsibilities. This leaves the eagle feeling disempowered and the owl overwhelmed. The manager's inability to realize that there is more than one way to drive success has a detrimental impact on both the employee and the manager.

This urge to control the way things are done is ultimately based in fear. We may have a fear of failure, which is common to eagles, or a fear of making mistakes, which is typical of owls. We may fear looking bad, which is characteristic of parrots, or fear not being accepted by others, which often defines doves.

The next time you find you are imposing your way on others, ask yourself, "What do I fear?" Then consider the possibility that the negative outcome of using the other individual's methodology may not be as real or significant as you believe it to be. Entertain the possibility that your need for control may actually create a worse outcome.

Remember, someone with a style unlike your own may approach a situation differently from you, but their way may be equally valid and, maybe, even better.

The Chameleon Student

Picture an Eagle who becomes the leader of every team he joins. From the outside, you may think he revels in his leadership abilities and enjoys taking charge. At first, this may be true. Over time, however, this Eagle comes to believe that other people do not pull their weight. This causes him to work harder than everyone else on the team. Each new project reinforces his belief that others lack leadership. This Eagle comes to resent the fact that if he does not take the lead, nobody else will step up, and the group will get a poor grade. Ultimately, he grows to dislike team projects because he feels compelled to take on the lion's share of work.

Just as Carl discovered in the *Summer Festival*, if you believe that *only you* can handle a certain role, you will be stuck playing that role everywhere. You can imagine the Eagle in the previous example lamenting, "Why do I always have to be in charge?"

Others can lead, but the Eagle believes that only he can lead the 'right' way. While others may handle a job differently than the Eagle, that doesn't mean they will be less effective.

Let's take another example with an outgoing Parrot. She always seems to be the one who delivers group presentations to the class while her teammates tend to do the research. Instead of wishing that others would present, this Parrot should appreciate her own abilities and be happy that she does not have to do the things that she either cannot do or does not like to do.

People tend to fall into different roles based on their style. Some people take charge. Others wait for direction. Some have an action bias and can't wait to get started. Others have a planning bias and don't want to do anything until it is fully mapped out. Each role is valuable. If you are better at one than another, that's great! You found your niche. Let others discover theirs.

Whether you're working on a school project or fundraiser for an acapella group, you will burn yourself out if you try to do everything by yourself. You may even grow resentful if you believe that no one else can play your role. Appreciate your strengths and respect the gifts of others. Don't impose your way of doing things on the people around you. Let your team members contribute in their own special way and everyone will shine. You are all likely to get better grades too.

- ASK PROBING QUESTIONS to gain a deeper understanding of different perspectives.

- LISTEN TO AND EMPATHIZE with the needs of others.

- RECOGNIZE THAT LEARNING AND GROWTH OCCUR when we are open to alternative ways of doing things.

- SEEK EXCELLENCE NOT PERFECTION and allow for the possibility of mistakes.

- RELEASE BLACK-AND-WHITE THINKING and consider the gray areas where alternative options live.

Fall

Spontaneity Day

Asweet, gentle mist hovered in the air as the autumn leaves began to turn. The parrots loved this time of year. The trees began to add touches of splendor to the forest, complementing the parrots' multihued contributions. The harvest moon, a stirring sight, was set to rise just after sunset. Tonight the moon is going to be bigger and brighter than usual, emitting an orange glow that will favorably highlight the forest's complete palette of fall colors.

The parrots were looking forward with great anticipation to an event that always took place on this day of the year. But not Carl. He was hoping for rain or, at the very least, a cloudy evening. Every year the weather had been perfect for this occasion, as if the parrots' optimism willed it to be so. "It never rains on a parrot," Ivory and her friends liked to say.

Tonight was the night that many migratory birds, including the geese and ducks, began their long journey to a warmer climate. Everyone in the forest supported the "migrators" by gathering together and cheering them on.

A brief afternoon shower gave Carl hope, but, predictably, the sky cleared up. The event would go on as planned. The forest dwellers gathered in the Great Field to get a clear view of the sky.

Everyone was there, including eagles, parrots, doves, and owls. The squirrels made an appearance, too, but concentrated mostly on the food.

As the sun began its descent, the parrots were the first to arrive at the field. They were excited to see their friends and wanted to spend as much time socializing with them as possible. Meanwhile, Carl braced for another evening of pointless small talk. To him, there was nothing worse than spending hours engaged in superficial conversation. He preferred having long, meaningful discussions, but this was not the place for that. Small talk was the agenda for the night.

As the first migrators took wing across the golden sky, the parrots' cheers could be heard across the land. The soaring geese honked in appreciation.

When Carl arrived at the Great Field, Simon was the first one to greet him. The owl was happy to see a familiar face and to have someone to talk with. After they chatted a few minutes, Dee joined the pair. The eagle asked them both what they had been up to lately, shared what she had been working on, and took off. The owl and the dove continued talking until Ivory popped into their conversation.

The parrot shared story after story, effortlessly flowing from one topic to the next. It was a marvel to behold. Ivory was a storytelling tour de force!

Loud cheers erupted from the crowd as another V-shaped gaggle crossed the path of the moon. Every time a bird crossed the moon, the onlookers shouted "Mooooooon!" and then took a sip of their drink. Nobody knew at what point this ritual began, but most feel certain it was started by a parrot.

Carl, Simon, and Ivory continued their conversation until Ivory had them both laughing hysterically. She then spied an old friend, promised to catch up with them later, and was gone.

Carl and Simon stood there dumbfounded. "Wow," the dove said. "That was impressive."

"You are telling me," Carl replied. "She seems to have an infinite number of stories, and they all sound funny or unprecedented."

Simon smiled, "No matter what topic comes up, Ivory always has stories, and they are usually quite entertaining."

"I wish I could do that," Carl admitted.

"Yeah, me too," Simon replied.

"I really dread these events. I never know what to say," the owl continued.

"I know what you mean."

Their conversation was briefly interrupted by loud cheers, then an even louder chorus of, "Moooooon!" The two friends each took a sip of their drinks.

"That does it," Carl resolved. "I am going to be more like a parrot. Look at them. They never worry about anything. Everything is either working out as planned or on the way to working out. They live carefree lives and don't stress the small stuff. From now on, it's all parrot all the time for me."

"Are you sure about that?" Simon questioned. "Parrots are quite impulsive. Are you ready for that?"

"How about this?" asked Carl. "I will start by being spontaneous one day a week. That will ease me into the change. Starting tomorrow, Sunday will officially be known as Spontaneity Day."

"That's great!" Simon replied, as he pondered the irony of planning for spontaneity.

The next day the sun rose bright and hot over Home. Carl woke up early, ate a light breakfast, and prepared for his first adventure. He placed his lunch into a satchel while at the same time acknowledging that his meal could have been part of his unscripted day, but . . . there was no need to be reckless. Carl was ready to launch himself into the blue unknown.

For the first time in his life, Carl was winging it. He did not know where he was going. Without a specific destination in mind, he wondered how he would know when to stop. "I'll figure it out on the way," he thought. From the beginning he flew like a bird on a mission.

As he rushed passed a family of doves, he waved a quick hello. He zipped by some parrot friends who were lost in conversation, but he kept going. He crossed the southern tip of the Great Lake and continued on.

"I get it," he realized. "I am in the moment. Of course, now that I am thinking about the moment, am I really still in it or just thinking about it?"

He pondered that thought until he realized not only had he lost track of time, he had also lost track of his whereabouts. Had he turned north at the lake or headed south? Was his course east toward Crystal Cave or west toward the Forbidden Swamp?

That's when panic began to settle in. "What is wrong with me?" Carl thought. "How does anyone live like this? I am an owl, not a parrot. I have no idea what I am doing."

In an attempt to gain his bearings, Carl stopped flying. He looked around but nothing seemed familiar. A group of squirrels carrying an inordinate amount of nuts rushed by. "Look at that," he thought. "Even the squirrels are planning ahead."

After a long, steady exhale, he tried to convince himself that everything was okay. "This is really no big deal. Someone will come along and find me before it gets dark, and if not, I will be able to figure this out on my own."

He reflected on the conversation he had had with Simon, the one that had initiated Spontaneity Day, and that's when he remembered. "Oh, no! I told Simon I would spend time with him today. I never miss the commitments I make to others. This is a disaster!"

Carl decided to reverse his course and see if he could find his way back to familiar territory. He crossed a recognizable stream and looked around. He noticed a few rotted branches, which triggered another realization. "I cannot believe this! Today I planned to remove the dead branches above the entrance to my hollow. There is no way that is going to happen now!"

He couldn't believe he had gotten himself into this confusing mess. Suddenly he strained to pinpoint a small voice he heard ahead of him. He stopped and looked around, but saw nothing. He was about to continue onward when he heard it again. "Carl," the voice called. "Over here."

If it weren't for Carl's keen owl hearing, the voice would have gone unnoticed. Because of the anxious and heightened state he was in, Carl heard every sound as if it were bouncing off of a canyon wall and echoing back to him. "Carl, this way," the voice instructed.

That's when his sharp eyesight kicked in. Just ahead of him—sitting on a small, gray boulder—sat Xenia and her young friend Xander. The chameleons had shifted their color to neon yellow so they could be seen. Carl swooped from his branch and landed with a *thud* beside them.

"What's wrong?" Xenia asked. "You look distraught."

After releasing an expressive sigh, Carl explained in detailed glory how he was seeking to add a measure of spontaneity to his life so he could be more like the parrots. He described how the experiment had caused him to get lost and how he had failed to meet commitments to himself and others. After he had finished explaining his predicament, he asked, "Xenia, can you point me in the right direction?"

"I'd be happy to," she grinned. "Pointing others in the right direction is my specialty."

Carl relaxed a bit as Xenia looked deeply into his bright owl eyes and said, "It looks as if you were being spontaneous today."

"I was trying to experience some parrot energy," the owl answered. "I thought that if I practiced the parrots' ways, I could master them and learn to let go of my need to control, well, pretty much everything."

Xenia smiled and said, "Carl, you can get comfortable with what's hard for you to do, but that doesn't mean you have to try to turn your weaknesses into strengths."

"But sometimes I feel as if my need to plan everything hurts me," Carl said.

"So work on being a little more spontaneous," Xenia suggested. "Let go of some control when it benefits you to do so. But don't put so much energy into mastering that new skill because it's not who you are. As long as you can be spontaneous when you need to, you'll be fine."

Carl understood what she meant. He had not felt like himself all day and could not imagine acting like this on a daily basis. He also knew that it would take a tremendous amount of work to change the controlling part of him. No matter how hard he tried, he would never be a parrot. He acknowledged there would be times when he could ease up on his need for control, and he vowed to work on that.

"And so you are headed in the right direction," Xenia concluded. The chameleon and her young apprentice spun around to continue on their way.

"Wait a second!" Carl called to them. "I still do not know how to get home."

"You're already there," Xenia grinned. She looked to Xander to point Carl in the right direction. The young chameleon proudly said, "Just ahead you will find a stream. Follow it until you see the Council Tree. I assume you know where to go from there."

The group heard a chorus of "Moooooon!" in the distance. The parrots were continuing to cheer on the migrators. As the chameleons disappeared into the landscape, the owl found his way home. And he laughed a bit at himself as he wondered if it wasn't too late to get productive and trim the branches on his tree.

Chameleon Wisdom

Weakness fixing is damage control, but it is not development. And damage control can prevent failure, but it will never elevate you to excellence.
—Marcus Buckingham and Donald O. Clifton

We can spend three things in life: money, time, and energy. When we invest our money, we seek to maximize our return. When we spend our time and energy working on personal growth, shouldn't we expect the same? Developing our strengths provides the best return on that investment.

Why do we expend so much time and energy trying to fix weaknesses that will have the least impact on our success? Perhaps it is because somewhere along the line it became politically correct to reframe weaknesses as challenges that need to be fixed or overcome. This idea prompts people to place their developmental efforts into turning liabilities into assets—a bad investment. It is more effective, instead, to focus on building our strengths.

This does not mean that we should completely ignore our weaknesses. In fact, we should expend some energy into developing our weaknesses so they do not hinder our future success. If something inhibits our ability to do our job or creates conflict with others, we should fix it. Acknowledge your weaknesses, but do not obsess over perfecting them.

In *Spontaneity Day*, Carl sought to let go of all controls and fly wherever the winds took him. He quickly discovered that his focus on his weaknesses inhibited his effectiveness. Whatever we focus on expands, so focusing on his weakness increased a feeling of incompetence. If Carl had concentrated on developing his strengths, he would have increased his self-esteem because confidence is grounded in our natural gifts. With Xenia's assistance, Carl realized he does not have to master being spontaneous. Instead, he has to get comfortable with being so when necessary.

Consider a dove in an office setting. He is reserved and does not like to speak in front of a group of people. During a meeting, a decision has to be made that would significantly affect his role. If he can endure the discomfort of sharing his concerns with the group, his needs will be met. But if he cannot, the team could make a decision that would make his job more difficult. The dove does not need to work on becoming a highly assertive person who lives his entire life candidly expressing his concerns openly to everyone he meets. However, it would serve him well to get comfortable enough with speaking up in meetings when it is critical to his job to do so.

Putting energy into developing our natural gifts empowers us because we are targeting behaviors that feed us. In turn, we reach higher levels of performance and accomplishment.

Greatness is not based on the absence of weakness, but rather, on living from one's strengths. Invest your time and energy in that which produces the greatest return on investment.

The Chameleon Student

As you progressed through elementary, middle and high school, you developed new skills. Some came naturally. Maybe you found it easy to memorize vocabulary and analyze literature. Other skills might have alluded you no matter how hard you tried to learn them. Perhaps math wasn't "your thing."

New skills feel unusually challenging to learn if you aren't innately wired for them. Consider how Parrots management their time. Since they often prioritize fun over work, they tend to hang out with friends before tackling school assignments or chores. Conversely, Owls are wired to study or clean their room first so they don't have to worry about it later. Parrots are more likely to pull an all-nighter to study for a test, whereas Owls can't imagine studying last-minute.

Can Parrots learn to master time management? Sure, but they have to worker harder at it than Owls who naturally structure and organize their time. Do Parrots *need* to become masters at time management? Not necessarily. Parrots need to become skilled enough at time management to earn good grades and succeed in a career.

In *Spontaneity Day*, the Owl tried to act more impulsively. The results were disastrous. Taking on unnatural behaviors inhibited natural abilities.

Don't be self-critical if you haven't mastered every skill there is to master. Focus on your strengths and identify weaknesses that are getting in your way. Develop those weaker skills to the point that they no longer inhibit your potential.

- ACCEPT THAT EVERYONE HAS WEAKNESSES. We are human.

- DEVELOP SKILLS based on your existing style rather than trying to develop a new style.

- LOOK FOR WAYS TO IMPROVE your weaker areas, but don't obsess on them.

- FIND OTHERS who have strengths in your weaker areas and either delegate to them or ask for their assistance.

- FOCUS ON YOUR TALENTS, not your faults.

- BE FLEXIBLE ENOUGH to display other styles when needed, but don't try to change who you are.

Squirrel!

"**I**vory, focus!" Dee commanded with eagle directness. "The committee meeting is almost over. Can you please pay attention for a few more minutes so we can get out of here?"

"Sorry 'bout that," Ivory laughed. She pointed her multicolored wing toward the ground and explained, "Those two squirrels are cracking me up."

Carl rolled his large eyes in aggravation.

"That big, gray squirrel just pulled a nut out of the ground, the same nut that the small, brown squirrel just buried. Then the brown one ran back and discovered an empty hole where his nut used be."

Dee just shook her head.

Ivory continued. "The brown one looked pretty angry. He spiraled up that tree until he reached the big branch over there. He then he made a leap to another branch located above the gray squirrel. The gray one didn't like that one bit, so she just puffed out her belly. Now they're arguing."

"So they're arguing," Dee stated. "Let's finish our meeting so we can leave. I have other things to do."

"I feel bad for the little guy," Simon said compassionately. "I'm sure he worked hard to find that nut, and then it was taken away from him in an instant. That's not nice."

"It has nothing to do with being nice," Carl declared. "Your statement offends my owl sensibility. The gray squirrel clearly violated the Squirrel Code of Conduct, which states that one squirrel cannot remove a nut buried by another, even if the original squirrel forgot where he or she had buried it."

"How do you know the Squirrel Code?" Ivory asked.

"Doesn't everybody know all of the rules of the forest?" the owl replied.

"I guess not," Ivory shrugged. "Any way, I think of rules as suggested guidelines."

Carl's jaw dropped.

Dee interjected, "At least the brown squirrel is standing up for himself. That's important. You can't let others walk all over you, or they'll just keep doing it."

"I think he should just let it go," Simon said. "There are a lot more nuts out there."

"Let it go! You would just let it go? That's madness!" Dee declared.

"I don't feel that one nut is worth arguing over," Simon responded.

Even though Ivory originally laughed at the mayhem, she was becoming increasingly uncomfortable with how the squirrels were treating each other. "As I watch the brown squirrel trying to get his nut back, I feel as though the gray squirrel took advantage of him, and that's not fair. I'm going down there to talk with that nut thief! What she did was wrong, and I'm going to tell her."

"Nooooooo!" Carl and Dee shouted simultaneously.

"They'll stop arguing in a minute, and they'll forget about the whole thing before our meeting is even finished," the eagle said.

"I can't imagine that the brown squirrel will just let this go," Simon worried. "It would take a long time for me to forget something like this."

"That makes no sense," Carl announced. "First you said the brown squirrel should not stand up for himself. Now you are saying he will likely hold on to his anger for quite a while. Those two things are contradictory."

"You got that right!" Dee proclaimed. "Simon has it all backwards. You should stand up for yourself, and then you should let it go."

Ivory was puzzled by what she was hearing. "This isn't about deciding whether or not to fight or how long you will hold a grudge. This is about social justice. When someone has been wronged, the right thing to do is insert yourself into the situation and stand up for them."

"But you don't even know this squirrel. That makes no sense," Carl protested. "It is better to look at the facts and determine who is right. Then act accordingly based on the data. According to my observations, the gray squirrel violated the Squirrel Code. Therefore, the brown squirrel should enforce the established rules."

"Let's all take a deep breath," Simon requested.

"I agree," Ivory said. "You know what real madness is? We are arguing about arguing!"

"I think it's good that we have different perspectives," Simon said. "None of them are right and none of them are wrong. They are just different because we are different."

"I see what you're saying," Dee confirmed.

The two squirrels were winding down their disagreement when Simon concluded. "I remember Xenia once telling me that we see the world through our own eyes, and what we see creates our reality."

Ivory asked, "So we can all see the same situation and each respond differently?"

"I believe that is right," Carl stated. "We see the world and react to it based upon who we are."

"I've always expected everyone else to see things how I see them," Dee acknowledged. "Maybe that's why you guys annoy me so much," she said with a grin.

Everyone laughed.

"That makes sense. I think you each have a valid viewpoint about the squirrels," the eagle announced with smile. "But we have a meeting to get back to, if that's okay with you."

As the meeting resumed, Dee noticed Ivory watching several bees pushing each other out of the way in order to claim a bright yellow flower as their own.

"Ivory, focus!" Dee directed.

Chameleon Wisdom

We don't see things as they are, we see them as we are.
—Anais Nin

We view the world through many lenses, such as culture, beliefs, experiences, and personality. They all impact how we perceive what happens around us. Just as a goldfish does not realize its view is distorted by the curve of the fishbowl's glass, we do not realize we are looking through our own lenses, which both create and distort our reality.

Our style shapes our perception of ourselves, others, and the world. It gives meaning to every conversation and event. The lens of our personality guides how we interpret what happens, why it happens, and how we think and feel about what has happened. Something that upsets one person can be no big deal to another. What thrills one individual can terrify someone else.

If we look through the eyes of a parrot, going on an unplanned adventure is exciting. That same experience may produce anxiety in an owl.

Without realizing it, we assume others see the world as we do, and we are surprised when they respond to circumstances differently. In *Squirrel!*, each bird was puzzled by how the others interpreted what they were watching.

What was offensive to one bird was a non-issue to another. Because the birds interpreted the situation through their own eyes, they did not understand each other's reactions.

We often misinterpret people's behavior because we use our own lens to understand their desires, expectations, motivators, and fears. Since we believe that we see the world as it is, unfiltered by own interpretation, we tend to overestimate the degree to which people will be aligned with our perspectives. Therefore, we expect the people in our lives to like what we like, want what we want, and react how we react.

Imagine a parrot eager to purchase a new car. He is excited to test drive a few vehicles and figures he can make a decision by the end of the day. His owl wife sees the situation differently. She would like him to conduct significant research before visiting various dealers. The parrot does not feel that level of preparation is necessary. The couple ends up arguing, not about which car to purchase, but rather how to make the decision. They see the situation differently and impose their views on each other.

Sometimes our lenses act like magnifying glasses that amplify the differences between ourselves and others. Blowing these differences out of proportion leads to personality clashes. People do things *for* themselves, not *against* us, so when others act in ways that push our buttons, we need to consider what needs they are attempting to satisfy. In most cases, their needs are *not* based on pushing our buttons.

With a little empathy, we can see the world through the eyes of others and increase our understanding and acceptance of them.

The Chameleon Student

As the birds learned in the *Squirrel!* fable, we see the world through our own lens and therefore respond to situations differently. Eagles see the world through a lens that is efficient, eager and enterprising. The Parrots interpret life as playful, positive and personable. Doves perceive experiences based on dependability, diplomacy and dedication. And Owls have a world view that is orderly, observant and organized.

Our styles color our experiences. Talking to recruiters at a job fair may be an ordeal to a Dove, while a Parrot may revel in talking about his varied accomplishments. The complex project that stresses an Eagle may be an exciting challenge to an Owl.

As we advance from middle school to high school to college, we usually encounter greater diversity. When we interact with people of different backgrounds and personality styles, we look through new sets of eyes. Our world becomes a rich tapestry of perspectives.

Don't just surround yourself with people who are like you. Join clubs that introduce you to an eclectic group of individuals. Try new hobbies to gain the opportunity to meet new and interesting people.

If you are studying to be an engineer and only join engineering clubs, such as the robotics team, you might surround yourself with fellow Owls. However, if you join a running club, theater or the marching band, you will meet those with a wide variety of personality styles and life stories.

Different perspectives don't threaten your way of being. They enrich your life. Each relationship will give you deeper insight into how Eagles, Parrots, Doves and Owls respond to the world. Likewise, a diverse group of people will introduce you to new identities, stories and lifestyles.

- RECOGNIZE THAT YOU HAVE A LENS through which you see the world, and that others have a different but equally valid lens.

- ASK YOURSELF, "What is the other person's motivation and desired outcome?"

- EMBRACE OTHER POINTS OF VIEW and ways of doing things.

- LET GO OF EXPECTATIONS, and be open to the needs of others.

- ASSUME OTHERS HAVE POSITIVE INTENTIONS to meet their own needs, not invalidate yours.

Observation Week

The autumn-tinted leaves blended effortlessly with the morning light. Fall was shining in all its glory, which meant that humans were on their way. With the heat of the summer behind them, people would soon invade the forest armed with binoculars, cameras, and backpacks.

Soon they would scatter throughout Home, though they usually congregated near the Great Lake and its adjoining pasture. The people came to observe the birds, but for the birds, it was an opportunity to observe the people. The birds liked to watch the human behavior up close and listen in on their conversations. Observation Week, as it had come to be known, allowed the birds to learn more about these elusive and unusual creatures.

On the first morning of Observation Week, the birds watched the foreign visitors spraying all sorts of substances on their bodies. The humans seemed to be inexplicably afraid of the sun and of bugs. Ironically, the sprays made them smell bad, which made them easier to locate and track.

The birds worked in pairs. Each couple contained two different types of birds. This allowed for diverse interpretations of human interaction.

On one team, Carl and Ivory joined forces for the day. Carl was pleased to be with such a vibrant companion. He thought that her vibrant colors would attract the attention of the humans and, as a result, afford the two birds greater opportunities to observe the people in action. Ivory was happy because she didn't have to take any notes. She knew that Carl would play that role.

Shortly after sunrise, the owl and parrot partners spotted their first human. Carl reviewed the three rules of Observation Week: "Be heard, but only occasionally. Be seen, but not too often. Be watched, but not for long. Most of all, do not do anything too unusual."

Their first quarry included one man and one woman. The owl and parrot maintained their distance. They didn't want to be discovered too soon. "We want them to get excited when they spot us. So let's not make it too easy," Ivory suggested.

As their prey approached, the birds could see that the man was carrying a small human on his back. The people spoke in hushed tones, but the baby squealed periodically, to the man's dismay. Carl's keen hearing picked up everything.

"What are they saying?" Ivory asked.

"The woman just told the man that she appreciates how well he organized their trip to the forest. I like him," Carl joked.

"Sure, you like him because he's an owl in human clothing!" Ivory smiled.

"Perhaps," Carl acknowledged. "In any case, the man is saying that he appreciates how she has entertained the child for the entire trip, singing songs and playing games."

"I like her," Ivory laughed.

"Of course you do. She is a parrot in human clothing," the owl concluded.

"And what beautiful clothing it is."

"Let me focus," Carl requested, as he tried to tune in again to their conversation.

The people continued walking through the woods, and Carl noticed how methodical the man was in his search for birds. When he periodically stopped to write in his journal, the woman entertained the child on his back.

Carl and Ivory did a good job of staying out of sight. They hid behind patches of leaves and large tree trunks. Occasionally, they would fly away and return, making certain to keep track of the visitors. The first time the woman spotted Ivory, she pointed loudly in the parrot's direction. This caused the child to squeal with excitement and the man to scold both of them.

The two birds occasionally allowed themselves to be seen, which kept the people interested. This gave Carl and Ivory a lot of time to watch the couple.

As the man took notes and photographs, Carl continued to be impressed by his attention to detail.

Ivory kept pointing out how funny the woman was. "Look at those faces she makes!" announced the parrot. "She's hilarious!" Her funny faces were making the child laugh in loud squeals of joy. This seemed to bother the man, but he did not say anything to her because he was too busy documenting their experience.

"Shhhhhh. They will see us," Carl cautioned. "And once they have seen enough of us, they will move on to find different birds."

After more than an hour of playing hide-and-seek with the humans, Ivory noticed that the male was becoming increasingly frustrated. As he kept trying to hush the woman, she kept trying to exclaim what a wonderful day she was having. She tried to encourage the man to relax and enjoy the surrounding nature, but he was too busy cataloging his experience.

Before long, the couple's banter turned into heated conflict. He was annoyed with her. She was annoyed with him. And they both seemed to be annoyed with the child.

"This is turning out to be a productive Observation Day," Carl noted. "But I must admit, I do not understand how these two humans joined together in the first place."

"I hear ya!" Ivory agreed. "They seem wholly incompatible."

"She must drive him crazy!" the owl exclaimed.

"I'll bet she has to do things exactly how he wants them done or he gets annoyed," the parrot hypothesized. "And he probably likes things done the same way every time."

"What is so bad about that?" Carl wondered. "That is how things get done properly."

Ivory huffed, "That's how things get done boringly."

Just then, a small voice emerged from the branch beside them. The owl and parrot were startled to discover Xenia and her newest student.

"Hey, Xenia and Xander," Ivory said. "Check it out—arguing humans!"

"Oh, is that what is happening here?" the wise chameleon grinned. "I thought I saw arguing birds."

"It must be contagious. We caught it from the humans," Ivory laughed.

Xenia smiled softly and turned her gaze to the owl. "Carl, you look puzzled."

"I am fascinated by these humans. I do not understand how this couple chose to pair."

"What do you mean?" the chameleon inquired.

"They are opposites, just like Ivory and me," the owl noted. "I cannot imagine why they did not select someone more like themselves to partner with. Wouldn't that help them get along better?"

"That's not always the case with humans," Xenia explained. "They are often attracted to their opposite. In fact, I regularly see parrot people paired with owl people."

"That makes no sense," Ivory declared.

"I also see human eagles matched with human doves," the chameleon added.

"That makes even less sense!" the parrot concluded. "How does that work?"

"Think about it like this," Xenia began. "When humans first meet, they appreciate gifts that are different from their own. In fact, it's those very differences that often create the initial attraction."

"I can see that," Ivory said. "I suppose that's why Carl and I are friends. I appreciate that he likes to do things that I find challenging . . . like track all the stuff we are supposed to record during Observation Week."

"I can see how two very different people can complement each other," acknowledged Carl. "Truth be told, I do appreciate how

Ivory adds serendipity to my world. Her spontaneity impresses me."

"If you listen carefully," suggested the older chameleon, "you can hear humans say things like, 'He completes me' or 'She's my other half.' "

"But if they are so perfect for each other, why were these two humans arguing?" Ivory asked as she pointed to the couple down below.

"Did they get along better when they first arrived?" Xenia probed, as if she already knew the answer.

"Correct," Carl answered.

"As the day has worn on, they have grown tired and frustrated," Xenia said. "Their differences are causing conflict. In a relationship, when times are easy and simple, such as when two people first meet, opposites attract."

"Or like when this couple's day first began," added Carl.

"Precisely," Xenia confirmed. "But during more complicated or stressful times, opposites repel."

"That must be inconvenient!" Ivory declared.

"Oh, it is," the chameleon replied. "When everything is going smoothly, they appreciate their differences. But when they need each other most, their differences can create friction."

"Um, we have a bit of a problem," Xander interrupted.

The young chameleon pointed towards to the humans below, "They're, uh, watching us."

"Well that must be quite an intriguing sight—an owl, a parrot, and two chameleons talking with each other on a branch," Xenia chuckled.

"It's time for us to go," Xenia stated. "You two enjoy the rest of your day. And try not to get caught chatting with anyone else. I believe that falls under the category of 'not doing anything that is too unusual.'"

"Now what do we do?" Ivory asked Xenia. But she asked too late. The chameleons had vanished. The humans below were still looking up toward Ivory and Carl.

Just then, the bushes behind the humans started to shake. The man grabbed the woman's hand, and they quietly fled the area. Ivory and Carl looked down toward the bushes to see what had scared the humans away.

Xenia and Xander jumped out of the bushes and landed on the ground. Xenia looked up toward the birds and gave them a thumbs-up and a smile. "I recommend you move on to another tree before they come back."

Carl and Ivory agreed. They flew away to find another human couple to watch on this year's first day of Observation Week.

Chameleon Wisdom

*We are sun and moon, dear friend; we
are sea and land. It is not our purpose
to become each other; it is to recognize
each other, to learn to see the other
and honor him for what he is: each
the other's opposite and complement.*
—HERMANN HESSE

Do birds of a feather flock together, or do opposites really attract? The answer depends on what we mean by "opposites." If we are referring to physical attractiveness, values, class, religion, race, and intelligence, more often than not, like attracts like. But when we are talking about personality styles or traits, quite often opposites attract.

In terms of the bird styles, the first pair of opposites is the eagles and doves. Eagles tend to be fast-paced, assertive, and independent risk-takers. Meanwhile, doves are deliberate, reserved, and group-oriented. They like to plan before taking risks. The second pair of opposites is the parrots and owls. Parrots are outgoing, social, big-picture oriented, and intuitive. Owls are reserved, private, detail-oriented, and logical.

It is important to note that any combination of styles can enjoy a joyful and lasting relationship. Opposites are not necessarily happier; they just tend to be drawn to each other.

So why is it common to hear people describe a partner as "my other half" or say that a spouse "completes me"?

Perhaps, if we tweak our language and think of opposites as complements, it would make more sense. Someone who complements our style provides us with the opportunity to experience a type of energy that we typically would not seek. Eagles, for example, might add intensity to a relationship, and parrots might add adventure. Doves might introduce compassion, and owls might offer precision. Our complement expands our horizons, enables us to see things differently, and transports us from familiar territory to uncharted waters.

A complementary partner may have qualities that we admire or wish we had. They help us learn, grow, and heal as their natural strengths subconsciously force us to deal with our deficiencies. An outgoing parrot, for example, can help an introverted owl in social situations. In return, the owl can help teach an impulsive parrot to stay organized so that life's responsibilities do not spiral out of control. A daring eagle might encourage a habitual and consistent dove to attempt new and varied activities. Meanwhile, a compassionate dove can teach a forthright eagle how to deal with situations that require a sensitive touch.

While connecting with our complement may have its perks, it can also have its challenges. When times are easy and comfortable, a partner with a complementary style can be endlessly fascinating, rich, and diverse. However, during stressful times, we are repelled by those who have a perspective different from our own. When times are tough, we do not have the time, energy, or patience to deal with someone who varies from our approach. When we are stressed, opposites don't just repel, they attack!

Perhaps that is why people of different styles often push our buttons in the workplace. At work there is constant pressure to perform. We are regularly faced with competing deadlines and ongoing changes in technology, procedures, and regulations. High-volume periods or busy seasons inevitably increase tension. In the office, we actually anticipate that there will be stress, which causes us to seek out people who think and act like we do. We want to get things done and wish people would see things the way we do.

Complementary styles can also repel each other at home. When couples have to deal with challenging situations or make significant decisions, they can enter into conflict and push each other away. Imagine an owl and a parrot trying to buy a new home. The owl wants to think through all of the pluses and minuses, while the parrot intuitively feels "this is the one!"

Imagine an eagle and a dove trying to coordinate their wedding. The eagle wants an unconventional event that reflects who they are as a couple, while the dove wants to satisfy the needs of everyone in attendance and wishes to adhere to a host of family and wedding traditions.

In *Observation Week*, Ivory and Carl watched an owl and parrot couple. In the early part of the day, when the pair was relaxed and eager to see the birds of the forest, their styles complemented each other. However, as the day wore on, the humans grew tired and frustrated. As their stress increased, their style differences created conflict.

While complementary styles often attract each other, individuals of the same style can be attracted as well. These like-minded individuals may validate each other's perspectives, and, therefore, have fewer disagreements. On the other hand, their similarities can get heated up and create friction. Two eagles may appreciate each other's candor, but each may vie to take the lead and dominate the other. Two parrots may appreciate each other's sense of adventure, but they may also compete for airtime during conversations. Two doves may value each other's support and compassion, but they might end up patiently waiting for the other one to take action when decisions need to made. Two owls might respect the other's attention to quality, but they may have competing ways of getting things done.

In the end, successful relationships depend less on what the differences are and more on how the differences are handled. The styles of two partners will not predict the couple's level of happiness or how long their relationship will last, but if the partners value their differences, they can create a well-rounded pair capable of achieving things that neither one could accomplish alone.

The Chameleon Student

When life is going well, we find excitement and novelty in different personality styles. But, as the birds (and humans) discovered in *Observation Week*, opposites can create stress during challenging times.

Sometimes at school, stress comes in predictable waves. You know that midterms, final exams and large projects will create anxiety. However, the challenges of joining new clubs, participating in sports, navigating a new campus, making friends and dealing with freedom can add unpredictable pressures.

Imagine working on a project that represents a large portion of your semester grade. You may be drawn to partnering with classmates who are just like you, as you believe that they will have a similar work style and therefore, you will have less conflict. An Eagle, for example, might choose other Eagles because they prefer to work independently, meet as little as possible and they don't get bogged down with details. Eagles say what they are going to do, they do it, and then they move on. An Owl team member might drive the Eagles crazy with exhaustive questions about the research, the report and the presentation. When the deadline approaches, the Eagles may feel like the Owl is slowing them down.

Even though the Owl's thoroughness may frustrate the action-oriented Eagles, the Owl can raise the quality of the project. It's natural to seek kindred personalities, but different styles add unique perspectives and skills. Plus, they may be happy to work on the parts of the project that you dislike.

Tap into the power of different styles. Instead of getting annoyed at people who want to do things differently, be thankful for their complementary ways of thinking and acting.

- EMBRACE DIFFERENCES as a way of having new experiences.

- MEET YOUR PARTNER HALFWAY by being willing to compromise.

- CAPITALIZE ON THE SKILLS that your partner has that you find difficult.

- DON'T JUDGE DIFFERENCES AS BAD, but rather, appreciate the benefits of what they offer.

Flight of the Groundhog

After a long journey, Ivory and Simon had almost reached Xandadu's Peak. Since the mountain rose so high above Home that it nearly touched the clouds, they had been able to see their destination for hours. With each passing minute, the peak grew larger and more imposing.

Xanadu was named after the wise chameleon teacher widely considered to be the greatest storyteller and wisdom-giver ever to grace their land. To this day, it is said that Xanadu watches Home from the top of the mountain, waiting to appear at just the right moment to teach another important lesson.

The Xanadu Theater sits at the base of the mountain. It is used to enact plays that embody the many lessons taught by Xanadu and his chameleon followers.

On this day hundreds of birds have huddled together, waiting for the amphitheater gates to open. They flew in from all over Home to watch one of the most ambitious performances ever attempted: *Flight of the Groundhog.*

Ivory and Simon circled the clearing beside the mountain and flew over the large crowd below. As the parrot and dove landed at the back of the crowd, Simon turned to Ivory and commented, "I wish we could have arrived a little earlier. I guess we'll be pretty far from the stage."

"Well, what can you do?" Ivory replied. "Sometimes ya gotta' stop along the way if something catches your eye."

"It's okay. We'll sit wherever there's a seat," said Simon.

After a long wait, they made it through the entrance and then inched their way to the back of the seating area. As they moved through the crowd, Ivory exchanged greetings with what seemed to be half of the audience. The dove could not believe how many birds his parrot friend knew.

Ivory was especially excited about this play because she had had a role in creating the costumes. Even though she had never had a chance to watch a performance, she had been told it was hilarious and had crazy special effects. Simon was looking forward to it as well. He had heard that the play was very touching.

As the show was about to begin, darkness fell upon the amphitheater. The crowd grew quiet as thousands of fireflies surrounded the stage. Then, in one mighty pulse of electricity, the theater exploded with light. The audience erupted in applause. The illumination revealed a stage set that resembled a three-dimensional map of the entire forest.

In the center was the Great Lake represented by a pool of water contained by a low, stone wall. At the back, a peak, formed out of a hill of dirt and some baby trees. In the front, the beach, created from a generous amount of silky sand. To the left, the ominous

Forbidden Swamp, fashioned from vines and muddy water. And to the right, the beautiful Crystal Cave, crafted from a variety of colorful crystals.

A small, gray dove dressed as a groundhog ambled onto the stage and stood between the sandy beach and the Great Lake. She looked at the sky and then glanced around the staged forest as if she were looking for something or someone. After she failed to find what she was seeking, she slumped down next to a tree, expressing profound sadness and solitude. Simon joined many others in the crowd who were voicing a sentimental, "Awwwww."

Ivory glanced at her dove friend as if to say, "You already feel bad for the groundhog? You don't know anything about her yet."

"She's upset," Simon said sadly.

As a bright yellow sign rose from the bottom of the stage, the fireflies increased the intensity of the lighting. The groundhog began to wander woefully around the forest. She was soon joined by a hilarious duo of eagles dressed as chipmunks. It was quite a sight. The chipmunks danced their way to the stage, wiggling their backsides as they performed what they called, "The Acorn Dance."

Ivory burst into hysterics.

Simon turned to gaze at the parrot.

"What? That's awesome! Just look at them," Ivory said.

"Yeah, it's funny," Simon replied blankly.

When the groundhog and the chipmunks began talking, the audience discovered that the young groundhog had been separated from her parents and was traveling the land, hoping to find them. Simon wiped a tear from his eye. "Oh, come on, Ivory. How are you not crying?" Simon asked.

"It's touching," the parrot conceded.

"But how are you not *feeling* anything?"

"I'm crying on the inside," Ivory responded.

Simon shook his head in disbelief.

The groundhog traveled throughout the land, meeting a collection of interesting characters, from owls dressed as bears to parrots dressed as chameleons. As the groundhog sought help to keep going, she received a gift of food here and a place to stay there.

Simon felt every act of compassion as if he were receiving it directly. As the play progressed, the groundhog gained strength. Soon the groundhog became the helper and not the one in need. She gradually transformed into a confident hero, providing support to whoever required assistance.

When the play reached the grand finale, the young groundhog slapped on a pair of wings and soared through the air. Ivory nearly exploded with laughter . . . and she couldn't stop. Even after the groundhog landed, she was still laughing. "It keeps getting funnier!" she giggled. "What is wrong with you, Simon? Isn't this the funniest thing you have ever seen?"

"I do find it funny," Simon responded. "I'm laughing on the inside."

Ivory, who was already having a hard time containing her giggles, found Simon's words to be utterly hysterical. "Well, if you think it's so funny," she said, "you should tell your face. Because you don't look like you think it's funny."

Behind the parrot and dove sat two owls, one white and the other brown. Both owls were listening to Ivory and Simon's running commentary. The owls were puzzled by what they had been hearing. The white owl noted, "I find it fascinating that they cannot read each other's emotions."

"Indeed," the brown owl said. "Listening to them is more interesting than watching the play. They seem to completely misinterpret each other's feelings."

"Why do you think that is?" asked the white owl.

"They are making assumptions based upon their own reactions and then drawing faulty conclusions," explained the brown owl.

"Tell me more," the white owl requested.

"Well, the parrot thinks, 'If it is funny, I laugh. So if you do not laugh, you do not find it funny.'"

"I see," the white owl affirmed. "And to continue that logic, the dove thinks, 'If it is touching, I cry. So if you do not cry, you do not find it touching.'"

"Exactly." Their conversation was interrupted briefly by raucus laughter. When it died down, the brown owl added, "I see your point, but it is not unreasonable to make assumptions based upon the data that is available."

"Ah! But that is when we introduce error into the equation," said the white owl, who had paused to look up at the towering peak above them. "If I recall correctly, it was the great Xanadu who once said, 'Do not project your emotions onto someone else's reactions.'"

"He was truly wise," the brown owl declared.

When the play came to an end, everyone stood in appreciation. Ivory turned to Simon and asked, "So what do you think?"

"I loved it," Simon replied. "The story was so moving."

Ivory concurred. "I loved it too. It was so funny!"

As everyone was exiting the theater, the brown owl turned to the white owl and concluded, "For the record, this play was funny, but I'm not sure it was as funny as the parrot thinks it is."

"I concur. The play was touching," the white owl noted. "But not as touching as the dove feels it was."

Chameleon Wisdom

*Real magic in relationships means
an absence of judgment of others.*
—WAYNE DYER

In our objective world, emotional reactions have clearly defined meaning. Laughing indicates something is funny. Crying indicates it is sad or touching. In *Flight of the Groundhog*, Ivory's laughter meant the play was funny. When Simon did not laugh, she *obviously* thought he did not find it humorous. At the same time, since Ivory didn't cry, Simon *clearly* construed that she did not find the play moving.

We interpret people's reactions based upon what we see. We also judge their reactions based upon what they would mean if we had that same reaction. We are the standard by which behaviors are defined and construed. We expect others to match our emotional intensity, and when they do not, we assume they do not feel that emotion as deeply as we do.

When eagles get aggravated, we see the strength of their conviction. If we do not match their intensity, eagles perceive that we are not as annoyed as they are. When parrots are excited and we do not match their level of enthusiasm, they assume we do not understand or appreciate how good something is. If doves become upset because someone has hurt their feelings, they presume we are insensitive if we are not as offended as they are. And if owls worry about something and we do not display the same level of concern, they suppose we must not be as committed to dealing with the issue as they are.

When someone else's emotional intensity does not match our own, we may assume that they are not aligned with our perspective. In the above examples, eagles expect a passionate display of emotion, while parrots expect enthusiasm. Doves expect empathy with their emotional needs, while owls expect us to join them in thoroughly assessing situations. If we do not meet the needs of others, they may not feel supported by us or believe that we care as much as they do.

Since all disappointment comes from expectations not being met, we set ourselves up for discontent when we expect the reactions of others to match our own level of intensity.

Consider a married couple consisting of an eagle and a dove, who are upset with each other. The eagle has a massive outburst. The dove remains silent but feels deeply hurt. Since the dove does not raise any concerns, the eagle assumes the dove is not bothered. Meanwhile the dove assumes the eagle is holding onto anger because she knows that if she had unleashed that much emotion, her anger would have lingered for quite a while. In reality, though, the eagle simply raised the issue and let it go.

It is very easy to project our interpretation of what a certain reaction means onto someone else's reaction. How we interpret other people's actions reveals more about who we are than who they are.

Consider a parrot who has a great idea while driving to work. He believes his idea will fix an issue that has plagued the organization for months. The parrot is brimming with excitement.

As soon as he arrives at work, he heads directly to his manager's office. His owl manager is engrossed in a project. She looks up from her desk with an expression that reads, *I am busy so make it quick.* The parrot does not waste any time sharing his idea. The owl listens intently as the animated parrot speaks enthusiastically and makes such optimistic claims as, *This will change everything!*

The owl manager takes a moment to consider the idea and then requests, "That could work, but there are a lot of questions that need to be answered before we move forward. Why don't you look into it and get back to me with what you discover."

The parrot leaves the office feeling utterly deflated. He was hoping for a level of reaction that matched his own. Instead, he received an assignment with a business-like acknowledgment that his idea was worth investigating. If the parrot had heard, instead, that his idea was an amazing one that could transform the company, he would have been energized beyond words. Since the owl did not convey what the parrot judged to be any measure of exuberance, he felt she must not have loved the idea. In fact, the parrot was not even sure that she liked it.

The parrot did something we all do all the time. He filtered his interpretation of another individual's response through the screen of his own personality style. It is hard for us to imagine that a reaction can mean something different when it is displayed by someone else, but it is important for us to consider the personality style of the source of the reaction.

The next time you feel concerned, hurt, or bothered by someone else's reaction, do not ask yourself, "What would I be feeling in order to elicit such a reaction?" Rather, ask yourself this: "Given the nature of this individual, regardless of his or her outward behavior, what is he or she likely feeling?" If you are uncertain, you can always ask.

The Chameleon Student

Whether you are starting a new grade or entering a new school, transitions to different environments create angst. In high school and especially college, you gain more autonomy. The tradeoff for that freedom is more responsibility and stress.

Some people internalize their anxiety, while others let it show. You may mistakenly assume that others handle stress the way you do. For example, if you always 'let it out,' you might conclude that a classmate who looks calm on the outside must be calm on the inside. That assumption can make you feel inadequate or inferior.

In *Flight of the Groundhog*, the birds discovered that we often project our emotions onto others. Consider a scenario in which you are taking a brutally difficult class. You feel confused and lost. The people around you appear to understand the material because they look relaxed. But just because others don't look concerned or confused that doesn't mean they aren't.

Don't compare your insides to someone else's outsides. Behind a calm face there may be anxiety. Others are probably in the same boat. Ask the people around you how they feel to see if they are experiencing the same challenges. You might be surprised.

- DON'T MAKE ASSUMPTIONS about how someone is feeling based on how you would be feeling if you had that same reaction. Always consider the source.

- CONSIDER PERSONALITY STYLE when making sense of others' behaviors.

- RECOGNIZE THAT EXPECTATIONS ARE THE SOURCE of disappointment.

- LET GO OF THE NEED FOR OTHERS to match your intensity of emotion. Someone might be feeling something deeply despite their non-reaction.

The Storm of All Storms

The wind howled throughout the day, and the late autumn leaves twisted wildly. As lightning flashed in the distance, booming thunder echoed throughout the land. Dead branches fell to the ground. Sharp *snaps* and dull *thuds* kept everyone's heads spinning.

Carl poked his head out of his tree hollow to assess the damage caused by a nearby crash when he heard the sound everyone dreaded. The Forest Alert System had been activated. A bird from the Westlands, the area west of Home, was the last bird in what had been a series of messengers. Her warning: The current storm was worsening, and more powerful winds were on their way.

As Carl watched the trees forcefully sway, often bending to the point of breaking, he wondered what else lay ahead of them on this ominous day. Through the relentless rain, he noticed something dark and large moving at a high speed . . . and it was coming his way. He stared at the brown blur until it came into focus. It was an eagle. No, wait. It was Dee, and she was battling strong winds as she struggled to navigate through the trees. Carl was accustomed to watching her surf the thermals high above the treetops, but these winds were impossible to ride.

When the eagle landed on a branch near Carl, the bough dipped under her weight. Skipping the usual pleasantries, Dee immediately dove into the crisis at hand. "From what I hear, the incoming storm is a monster. The Westlands are being pounded with rain. Floods are washing away the topsoil, and mudslides are ripping trees from their roots. Everyone is scrambling for cover. We need to prepare."

"Sounds like it's going to be a bad one," the owl replied.

"I just came from the Council Tree, and I have been appointed to coordinate the preparations. I selected you to be my assistant. Congratulations."

"Uh, thank you," the owl stuttered. "I am glad to help."

"Good. Let's begin. First, I need you to contact the parrots. They are responsible for communicating the strategy, once we determine what that will be. Second, talk to the other owls and have them draw up a plan. On second thought, scratch that. The owls will take too long. I'll create the plan."

Carl was a bit offended that Dee insulted his fellow owls, but he put that aside for now because there was much work to be done.

"Should I contact the doves?" Carl asked. "I can ask them to prepare to support anyone who gets displaced during the storm."

"No time for that. We'll worry about damage control later," the eagle said as she flapped her mighty wings and disappeared.

"Okay, then," Carl replied to the empty space where Dee had just stood. "I guess I will go talk to the parrots. Though I am not quite sure what I am supposed to tell them."

The wind was pushing and pulling Carl in every direction as he made his way to his colorful friends. On arriving, he could only tell them that it was their job to convey the storm strategy to everyone else, and that they should stand by. The parrots were eager to play their part.

As trees twirled beneath the dark gray sky, and violent winds tore leaves off branches and sent them swirling through the air. A wall of rain pelted Carl as he fought his way back to his tree. He felt responsible for keeping everyone safe, and uncomfortable at not understanding the plan.

Shortly after Carl returned to his tree, Dee arrived. Before she even touched down, the eagle began dictating orders. "Here's what we are going to do. First, we will move everyone further south, where the storm is not as severe. The base of the large falls, just north of the pine forest, will be our meeting place. When we get there, we'll take attendance and determine if we need to move further south. If we do, we will identify someone who has the energy and speed to fly ahead and identify trees with large leaves that can act as a canopy for the smaller birds. I don't know if we have enough food to weather this event, but we'll figure that out when . . ."

"Hold on. I have a question," Carl interrupted. He was feeling uneasy about Dee's strategy. "How do you know that the storm will not be as bad in the south? When we were hit with a big storm two years ago, the south received more rain than the north did, and they had terrible flash flooding and landslides. Have you received additional information about what is coming?"

"No," said Dee, "but in a crisis you sometimes have to make assumptions. My experience tells me that I am right. Besides, this is not a good time to doubt leadership. This is a time for action."

"Whoa. Wait a second," the owl requested. "I am not challenging your leadership. I just want to make sure we have thought this through. Is that your entire plan, or is it an overview?"

"That's all of it," Dee declared. "What more do you need? Head south and I'll see you there."

Carl was dumbfounded. Surely there had to be more. He stared at Dee in stunned silence.

Dee took Carl's lack of response as acceptance of the plan, so she continued. "I will be part of the advance team. I'll head south and establish a base. You make sure the parrots tell everyone where to go."

And she was off.

Carl shook his head in disbelief. With great effort he made his way back to the parrots. He tasked them with announcing the plan, such as it was.

As Carl made his way to the pine forest, he thought about the storm and their options. He visualized their destination, and he had an epiphany. "We are heading south to seek cover in the pine forest, but pine trees do not have leaves! Where does Dee think we are going to get protection from the wind and rain? This will not do. This will not do at all."

As he continued to fly, the owl watched the approaching black sky spread like a blanket across the forest. The rain had softened slightly. When he arrived at the meeting place, Dee seemed a bit smug that her plan was working. Carl approached the eagle and asked, "Now what?"

"The storm is still coming this way. We need to head further south."

Dee turned away from the owl and hopped up to a higher branch. She called for everyone's attention, and the group quickly grew silent. "We can't stay here. We need to keep moving. Ivory, you fly ahead and scout out a safe place for us to shelter from the storm."

"Got it," Ivory confirmed as she leapt into the shadowy sky.

"Now, follow me!" Dee shouted over the growing wind.

No, not again, Carl thought. *We need to think this through.*

Without another moment's hesitation, the owl summoned his courage and let loose a mighty shout. "Deeeeeeeeeeeee!"

To the owl's surprise, the eagle heard him and wheeled quickly around to return. When Dee arrived, she snapped a quick, "What?"

Everyone froze.

"Dee, can I speak with you for a moment?"

The eagle stared intensely into Carl's eyes without saying a word. The owl quickly began, "Your plan is not complete. Think like an owl for a moment. We need more details that include step-by-step instructions for each of us to follow. We need to carefully consider our strategy and determine precisely where we are going. I'd also recommend that we assign group leaders who will be responsible for . . ."

"Carl, you think like an owl, but I'm an eagle, and that's not what I do. I was chosen to lead everyone through the storm, and so we're going to do it my way."

"But I just want to discuss . . ."

Lightning cracked nearby, followed by an immediate *boom*. The raindrops grew bigger and began to hit harder. The storm was worsening.

"I already gave you clear instructions. Head south and find cover. As for assigning roles, here's one for you. Get behind the group and bring up the rear."

Before Carl could utter another word, Dee commanded, "We can talk about this when we get further south. I know what I'm doing." Once again Dee announced, "Let's go!" With a powerful pump of her wings, she launched herself into the threatening darkness.

The owl sheltered his eyes with his wing so he could better see through the pummeling rain, but all he could make out was the eagle's fuzzy outline traveling away from him. As he watched all of the other birds get airborne, he remained on a branch thinking about what to do next. Watching his bird friends dodge leaves and falling branches prompted his decision to talk with Dee.

Carl was accustomed to making sharp, quick turns in the forest. Dee was not. Though it would take all his skill to navigate the deep woods and catch up with the eagle, he had to try. As Carl pressed against the wind, he thought about what he would say to Dee when he reached her. He acknowledged how much he appreciated her ability to handle a crisis without panicking, and he reflected on how he valued her willingness to take charge and make tough choices. Logic told him that she was the right one for this job, but her strengths seemed to be working against her. The eagle's desire to be in control had closed her off to the ideas of others. Her decisiveness could potentially make her reckless.

The wind whistled through the trees as bursts of lightning illuminated the forest. Dee's large wings slowed her down, which gave Carl the opportunity to catch up. As he watched the eagle repeatedly adjust her path based on ever-changing airstreams, he realized that he needed to shift his approach to her.

In a flash of insight, Carl recognized that he was treating Dee like an owl, not an eagle. He was trying to change how she acted when, in reality, the only thing he could truly change was how he dealt with her. Talking about plans and clarifying roles wasn't going to get him anywhere with Dee. Those were his strengths. He needed to adapt his message so it made sense to Dee, and encourage her to maximize her own abilities. This wasn't going to be easy, but so much was at stake.

When Carl approached Dee's right wing tip, she whipped her head around to see who was there. As thunder boomed around them, Carl tried to talk to Dee, but there was too much noise for her to hear him. The owl pointed to a nearby tree and signaled the eagle with his eyes to set down there. Dee could not imagine what Carl wanted, but she assumed that if he was motioning her to stop, it must be important. Dee gestured to everyone that they were going to take a quick break. Even though the group had not traveled far since their last stop, most of the birds were happy to rest their tired wings.

Carl landed first, and Dee slammed down beside him. The owl heard a sharp crack from the branch he settled on, but he disregarded it as the least of his problems. "Why did we stop?" Dee snapped.

The owl stood tall to address her as another eagle would. He confidently looked into her eyes and said, "Dee, I know you are on a mission to get us all to safety."

"That's right," she affirmed.

"You are driven to achieve success, and I appreciate that. But I'd like to share a concern that I think may prevent you from accomplishing your goal. Are you open to hearing it?"

"Yes, but make it fast. We've got to get moving."

So far, so good, Carl thought.

The owl continued, "Xenia once explained to me that I was overusing my strengths, which turned them into weaknesses. In my case, my desire for accuracy paralyzed me from making an important decision."

"Well, I don't have *that* problem," Dee observed proudly.

"Decisiveness is not your issue," Carl agreed. "But we both overuse our strengths, thus turning our greatest assets into our greatest liabilities. My perfectionism made me stuck. Your desire for action is making you closed and potentially careless."

Dee softened her tone. "So you're saying I am not listening to you and by not hearing what you have to say, I may be preventing our success?"

"Exactly!" Carl declared.

Dee spoke a little quieter and slower. "I am just trying to accomplish this goal as quickly as possible. I guess all the excitement about the storm has turned me into a super eagle." She paused for a second and then clarified, "And I don't mean that in a good way."

Carl's smile was followed by a brief silence. He was pleased that he had found a way to convey his concerns to Dee. The eagle summarized, "So to recap, I should not overuse my strengths. Got it. I'd love to talk more about this, but that lightning is getting close, and we've gotta go."

"If I may be so bold," Carl interjected before Dee could tell the group it was time to depart. "You just did it again. We need to act decisively, but before we do, can we take a couple of minutes to consider a few elements of the plan before we implement it?"

The eagle took a deep breath to slow herself down. "This is going to take some practice. Okay. What are your concerns?"

It didn't take long for the pair to assess the plan. After two minutes, they set off toward a nearby cave that Carl once visited.

They waited out the tempest from within the safety of the cave. When the clouds and the danger had passed, the eagle and owl were elated that the "Storm of All Storms," as it had come to be known, did not take anyone's life, even though it had caused a lot of damage. Dee and Carl were treated as heroes who acted quickly and thoughtfully to save the day.

As Dee and Carl returned north, they could see the tremendous destruction that had been caused by the storm. What had once beautified the forest as towering trees lay smashed on the ground in pieces. Branches were strewn across the forest floor, and rivers of mud flowed throughout the land. As the two friends passed over the Great Lake, Dee glanced down and saw their reflections on the water. She thought about everything that had happened and said, "That was pretty exciting, huh?"

Carl chuckled. "I think we define 'exciting' a bit differently. For owls, solving a challenging puzzle is exciting. Dealing with an unpredictable storm bearing down on us and feeling like we do not have a plan is anxiety provoking!"

"You like challenging puzzles? It sounds like figuring out how to handle me as I overused my strengths was a challenging puzzle," Dee acknowledged.

"I guess it was," Carl replied.

"And you solved it. You slowed down an overzealous eagle and got her to listen."

Carl nodded slowly.

"You can thank me later for making your life exciting," Dee smiled.

"But . . . you . . . oh, forget it," Carl grinned sarcastically. "Thanks."

Chameleon Wisdom

Everyone thinks of changing the world,
but no one thinks of changing himself.
—LEO TOLSTOY

Think about a personal habit you would like to change. If one does not come immediately to mind, reflect on a previous New Year's resolution. Most people put effort into changing a habit for a few days or maybe even a week or two . . . only to revert back to the previous behavior afterward.

Now identify someone else—a spouse, child, or coworker—who has a habit that you would like to change. If you have put forth any effort to encourage them to alter that habit, you have discovered how difficult it is to change someone else. One of life's hardest lessons to learn is this: It is challenging enough to change ourselves, but it is practically impossible to change someone else.

You cannot change your child's annoying taste in music. You cannot change your spouse's neatness or lack thereof. And most of all, you cannot change someone else's personality style. We can lecture them, scold them, and highlight their shortcomings, but those tactics only lead to *our* disappointment and *their* resentment.

While we cannot push others into a different personality style, we can pull them in the direction of their own. Rather than trying to change other people, we can draw the best out of them by helping them capitalize on their natural strengths while, at the same time, not overusing their innate gifts.

In *The Storm of All Storms*, Carl tried to change Dee's behavior by attempting to get her to act more like an owl. He failed miserably until he realized he needed to honor Dee's style and help her to become the best eagle she could be. When Carl adapted how he spoke to Dee, she became more effective and he became less anxious. Dee was overusing her innate strengths. Carl brought her back into balance. He helped turn her into a great eagle rather than a mediocre owl.

When strengths are overused, they become weaknesses. An *eagle's* natural assertiveness turns into aggression. Directness hardens into bluntness and insensitivity, and their ability to take charge becomes domineering. A *parrot's* optimism turns into unrealistic expectations and impracticality. As parrots overuse spontaneity, they become scattered, and their abundance of enthusiasm appears superficial and over-the-top. *Doves* become passive. Their need for consistency creates resistance to change, and their desire for harmony causes them to become too lenient and permissive. *Owls* overuse their analytical skills and become indecisive. Their need for perfection causes them to become too critical. Their focus on the task drives them to detach from people.

When we overuse our own strengths, the stress eventually passes, and ultimately, we return comfortably to our successful style. However, when others overuse their style, we sometimes try to change them.

Imagine a dove who wants to give feedback to her owl spouse. The dove is unhappy that the owl is inflexible with the rules they have imposed on their children. One day, their child arrives home late, and the owl immediately applies strict consequences. The dove feels that, in this instance, there were extenuating circumstances, and they should have been more lenient.

The dove approaches the owl with an impassioned plea to reduce the child's punishment, but the owl simply reiterates the rules. The dove speaks to the owl in the language of the dove, making statements like, "You need to be more sensitive and compassionate." She also says things that run counter to the language of the owl, such as, "Not everything is so black and white."

The dove would have had more success changing the owl's behavior if she had honored his innate owl style while she was trying to get him to tone down his overuse. Instead, she tried to get him to exhibit dove behavior. She would have accomplished more if she had said, "I understand that we have rules and they need to be followed. I also recognize that it is important for parents to enforce the rules. However, if we impose consequences without considering all the facts, we may trigger our child to rebel against what he feels is unfair treatment, which could prompt him to violate more rules in the future. Perhaps we can look at the specifics of this incident and determine an appropriate response."

We may not be able to change others, but we can change the way we deal with them. When we try to alter someone's fundamental nature, we are rarely effective. And worse, the attempt can damage the relationship. But when we help others become the best version of themselves, our efforts can build a stronger connection and help them to shine.

The Chameleon Student

The more effectively you communicate, the more successful you will be in any career. You can take your communication skills to another level by learning to talk to others how they listen. In *The Storm of All Storms*, Carl learned that if he reflected Dee's Eagle style back at her, she would pay attention.

Imagine the power of communicating to teachers in their styles. If you have an Eagle professor who calls on people during class, answer directly and assertively. Your Parrot teacher may appreciate a bit of humor and enthusiasm, while the Owl might want the logic behind your answer. Dove teachers are unlikely to put you on the spot. If they do, answer with sincerity and talk about the personal impact of the subject.

Inevitably, you will collaborate, live or work with people of different styles. Communication is often the source of conflict between different personalities. If you learn to speak each style's language, you can satisfy style-driven needs.

Imagine that you are the president of a language club and need to motivate your members to support a fundraising activity. If you want to motivate the Eagles, tell them how the money will impact the recipients. It might not hurt to mention that the Eagles can add the initiative to their college application or resume. Engage the Parrots by highlighting how fun it will be to raise money together. Paint the picture for the Doves how much the recipients will appreciate the donations. Be sure to share real-life examples of the good that the club will accomplish. For the Owls, emphasize that you value their organizational abilities and need their help to run an effective campaign. Tell Owls the exact details of how the funds will be used.

Mirroring the language of other styles will help you connect with people, communicate persuasively and lead gracefully. The ability to influence others is at the heart of leadership. Discern the styles of the people around you, then be the chameleon and flex to what the person or situation requires. When you meet people's needs, you are more likely to get yours met as well.

- NOTICE YOUR JUDGMENTAL THOUGHTS about others. Instead of thinking about how you would like to change them, think about how you can positively impact them.

- YOU WOULD NOT WANT PEOPLE TO TRY to change you, so consider how others feel when you to try to change them.

- CHANNEL YOUR ENERGY into altering your approach rather than trying to change someone's style.

- SEEK TO TONE DOWN OVERUSE rather than change someone completely.

- HELP OTHERS TO BE THE BEST they can be, but don't try to change them to be more like you.

Winter

Mudslide

Because of a heavy rainstorm, Dee, Ivory, Simon, and Carl had rescheduled their Council committee meeting. After working through several issues, they were happy their gathering was finally coming to a close. With all their business now completed, Ivory announced it was time to celebrate.

As she flew to a nearby tree to retrieve something, Carl asked, "What are we celebrating?"

Ivory shouted over her shoulder, "Life!"

When she returned to the Council Tree, she placed a container filled with a pungent, bluish-yellow mixture in the center of the group.

The parrot explained that she had flown for hours to a secret location in order to find an ancient exotic plant. From the roots of that plant, she had brewed this special concoction for her friends. Ivory was eager to share her creation.

The parrot carefully poured some of the liquid for each of her friends. She sensed their hesitation to taste it, so she encouraged, "Don't worry. It won't hurt you. Enjoy!"

They all picked up their drinks and, in an act of solidarity, simultaneously sipped their drinks. The birds' eyes grew wide.

With the compassion of a dove, Simon spoke first. "Ivory, this is very good. Thank you for taking the time to prepare this for us."

Dee, the feisty eagle, looked as if she was about to say something to the contrary when Simon shot her a look. Dee thought better of her plan and just smiled.

As soon as Ivory turned to Carl to get his opinion, the forest received another urgent warning. For the second time in a few days, The Forest Alert System had been activated. The message was being transmitted to the Council members by an out-of-breath dove who had come down from the north. "Mudslide . . . on . . . Xanadu's . . . Peak."

Carl was about to ask the dove if she knew anything else about the mudslide when he remembered that, according to the System rules he amended last year, all messages had to be five words or fewer in order to increase accuracy. He was now beginning to regret that requirement.

The mudslide was personal to the owl. Last year he had studied Xanadu's Peak with highly sensitive equipment and determined there was a low mudslide threat in that area. While the Council had previously recommended to the ground and tree dwellers in the area that they should relocate, Carl's report encouraged many to stay. He hoped that no one had been hurt today because of his report. He had to go check it out.

Dee stood tall, as eagles tend to do in the face of danger, and announced that she would join her owl friend. After Carl quickly packed a few measuring tools, the two friends flew swiftly to the unfolding disaster.

Meanwhile, Simon and Ivory remained back at the Council Tree so they could coordinate a rescue effort, if one was needed. Simon was worried about his friends, but he was even more concerned about injuries to those who lived at the base of the mountain. Ivory called on her innate optimism to reassure Simon that everything would be fine, but Simon was not convinced.

When the owl and the eagle arrived on the scene, they couldn't believe the extent of the devastation. Though the rainstorm had passed, a large mass of gooey muck was barreling down the southern slope of Xanadu's Peak. Large boulders were being sucked into a giant mud river overflowing with rocks, vegetation, and water. Piles of rubble were left in the mud's wake, and a mass of toppled trees created a new stripped and swerving path. The mud was moving straight to the Xanadu Amphitheater.

Calls for help echoed throughout the valley. Carl and Dee didn't know where to go first. Survivors caked in mud emerged from the forest. Dee flew to the top of the mountain for a bird's-eye view of the situation. That's when she saw it. A young weasel was being swept away in the mudflow. Dee gasped. When she was a young eagle, she had been caught in such a flow and had nearly drowned. Had it not been for a resourceful dove who had used a large vine to save her, Dee would not be here today.

The eagle summoned her courage and rapidly descended toward the weasel. Her heart raced as she got closer and closer to the unfortunate critter. She circled him for a bit, but she kept making larger and larger circles instead of banking in to make smaller ones. The weasel reached up for help, but Dee kept circling. Something inside her was pushing her away.

A nearby parrot saw what was happening and swooped in to save the day. With the mud-covered weasel secured to his chest, he made a jubilant victory lap before gently touching down beside the frightened weasel's relieved parents. As the reunited family hugged, everyone along the mud bank cheered . . . except for Dee.

When the eagle returned to her owl friend, she saw him surveying the extent of the damage. He was busy checking and rechecking his findings. Perhaps he didn't even notice what had happened.

Carl had just concluded that the unprecedented amount of rain must have saturated the earth. That caused loose dirt to mix with water to form mud, and all of this happened too quickly. Gravity kicked in and pulled the masses of wet soil down the slope.

"How could I have missed this?" Carl wondered aloud.

"Hey, we all make mistakes," Dee replied, happy to discuss anything but what had just transpired.

The owl reached into his bag and pulled out a measuring instrument. It only took a moment for him to realize that the equipment had been calibrated incorrectly, thereby causing all of his previous data to be wrong. It was hard for Carl to imagine that he made an error of such great magnitude, but he could not deny what he was looking at.

Carl explained the problem to Dee, who was still so embarrassed by her failure to save the weasel that she didn't tell Carl what she was really thinking. If Carl had checked his equipment, none of this would have happened.

Carl, too, was at a loss for words. He had been stunned when he noticed Dee's attempt to rescue the weasel, and now he was ashamed of his own actions. As the owl packed up his gear, Dee said quietly, "The wind was rough down there. A parrot with a wingspan smaller than mine was able to rescue a weasel from the mud. His diminutive wings allowed him to make the tight turn needed to grab the little fellow. You do know that I would have done it if I could have, right?"

Carl just nodded.

The pair headed back to the Council Tree without saying another word. When they arrived, Carl explained to Simon and Ivory how faulty equipment had created inaccurate measurements in last year's study. Ivory didn't seem to need all the details. She was just happy they had returned and relieved that everyone was okay.

However, the longer Carl spoke, the more agitated Dee became. She kept thinking that she would never have been placed in the awkward position of trying to rescue the weasel by herself if Carl had not made such a critical mistake in the first place. Ultimately, the eagle couldn't take it any longer. "You know, Carl, if you had carefully checked your equipment before you made your measurements, the Council would not have declared 'minimal danger' in this community and none of this would have happened."

"Excuse me, Dee," Carl snapped. "But I did not make a mistake. The equipment was not set correctly."

"And who had used the equipment?" the eagle shot back.

"I think you are upset because you were too afraid to fly close enough to the mudslide," accused Carl, as he abruptly changed the subject. "I believe you could have saved that weasel and that your version of the facts lacks a factual basis."

"Are you saying that I am lying?" Dee glared.

"Hold on everyone," Simon interjected. "Let's all calm down. None of this is anyone's fault. And nobody is calling anybody a liar. I'm sure that both of you did your best today, and that's all we can ask of anyone."

It was only then that Dee and Carl noticed it was no longer just the four of them standing on the branch on the Council Tree. Between Simon and Carl stood their old friend, Xenia. The chameleon's apprentice, Xander, watched silently from a nearby tree.

After some quick pleasantries, the chameleon cleared her throat and offered, "May I shed some light on the matter?"

"By all means," Simon requested.

"Can I be completely honest?" she questioned.

A chorus of "of course," "yes," "absolutely," and "sure" gave her permission to proceed.

"Very well, then," she continued. "I sense that a bit of deception has taken place here today. But we all engage in deception every now and then."

"So you agree that I lied?" the eagle snapped.

"Dee, we all stretch the truth at one time or another," the chameleon explained.

"Well, I wouldn't blame equipment for my inadequacy," Dee insisted.

"Perhaps," Xenia acknowledged, "but that's because your personality is different from Carl's. Who we are drives why we deceive others."

A group of fast-moving squirrels whizzed by the birds carrying an abundance of nuts. The friends froze in wonder until the squirrels passed, and then they turned their attention back to the chameleon. Recognizing that the group needed more information, Simon asked Xenia to explain.

Xenia continued. "Xander and I couldn't help but overhear your conversation earlier today when Ivory offered each of you a bit of her special drink. Xander is right over there, by the way. Don't try to look for him. He's practicing blending into the colors of a beehive, so I don't think we should call attention to him."

Ivory smiled as she tried to catch a glimpse of the beehive-colored chameleon. "Hey, if I knew you two were there when I was pouring the drinks, I would have offered you some."

"Oh, that's quite all right, Ivory," the chameleon grinned. "But thank you for thinking of us. Besides, I'm not so sure that everyone enjoyed it as much as you did."

"What do you mean?" the parrot asked. "They all loved it!"

Xenia caught Simon's eyes before speaking. "Simon, did you enjoy it?"

Simon didn't know what to say. He tried to speak but couldn't seem to summon the right words.

"That's all right," Xenia said, letting him off the hook. "You see, like the rest of us, doves tell what we like to call 'white lies.' They sometimes obscure the truth so they don't hurt others' feelings."

Simon gave a subtle nod to acknowledge the truth spoken by Xenia.

Ivory then turned to Simon and said, "Don't worry about it, Simon. Honestly, this batch wasn't my best."

Xenia shifted her gaze to the parrot. "Ivory, as for this mysterious root you gathered, I am quite familiar with it. If I am correct, it's easily obtained not too far from here."

For once, Ivory didn't know what to say. Simon broke the uneasy silence. "But the distance did make it seem more mysterious."

"Parrots often embellish or exaggerate the facts," Xenia explained. "And as Simon just said, the distance does make for a better story."

Ivory nodded. "I suppose that's true."

"Now then, let's get to the bottom of this mudslide situation," the chameleon stated. "Dee, you do not like to appear weak, do you?"

"Heck no!" the eagle confirmed.

"And you don't want anyone to think that you lack courage, do you?"

"Absolutely not," Dee replied reflexively.

"So could it be that you were not completely forthright about what happened when you were trying to save that weasel?"

"Well, maybe not," conceded Dee.

Carl shot the group a judging glance. "I, for one, am very concerned about all of this deception. I would never . . ."

Xenia raised her right palm to silence Carl before he dug himself into a hole. "Carl, are you upset with yourself that you did not properly calibrate your equipment before surveying the mountain?"

"I suppose I am," admitted the owl. "I don't like providing faulty data."

"Is it uncomfortable for you to admit that you have made a mistake?"

"It is. I want others to be able to rely on me," Carl said.

Simon turned to the owl and said, "But we would never think that you are unreliable."

Carl returned a thank-you nod and stated, "I appreciate that. Nevertheless, my first step to regaining your trust will be to support the cleanup efforts."

Xenia summarized, "We are all practiced at the art of deception. And who we are determines why and how we deceive ourselves and others."

The chameleon motioned Xander to move away from the bees before they noticed him. She then walked over to Ivory's strange brew and inhaled a whiff of the substance. She poured several droplets onto a leaf and tasted it with her tongue. She gave the group a big smile. Just before she faded into the tree, she said, "Delicious!"

Chameleon Wisdom

I've tried to do away with lying in my life in the last few years, but it's hard.
—Louis C.K.

Let's set one thing straight right from the start: Everyone lies. In fact, the average person lies several times a day. But before you get defensive, this statement refers to white lies typically borne out of kindness, not lies intended to deceive or harm. In fact, people often tell white lies to be polite or to protect the feelings of others.

White lies may be told to maintain privacy or foster positive relationships. We may tell these untruths to entertain, embellish, or exaggerate. Sometimes white lies are even told to boost the self-esteem of others or maintain our own self-confidence. While each of us tells white lies for different reasons, fear is the common underlying driver. Some people may fear looking bad, while others may fear upsetting someone or damaging a relationship.

We all have a self-image that we strive to maintain, and we want others to see us as we see ourselves. We tell white lies to protect our image, and we guard against projecting anything that runs counter to the way we wish to be seen. The particular fear that drives a white lie is based, in part, on our personality style.

In *Mudslide*, Dee sees herself as a strong and confident eagle. She does not want to project that she has fear or weakness of any kind. This self-image drives her to tell a white lie so that she is not seen as someone who lacks courage or experiences failure. Eagles like to cut their own path and take ownership of their destiny. Sometimes they stretch the truth to get what they want. To them, the ends often justify the means. If they fail, they may shift the blame to factors they could not control. Imagine a workplace eagle who says, "I would have achieved my goal if only that other department would have gotten me the information sooner."

Like Dee, Carl also told a white lie in *Mudslide*. As an owl, his self-image is based on his ability to do things accurately. He sees himself as careful, compliant, and consistent. As such, he lied to protect the perception that he can be trusted to do things properly. From his owl perspective, others rely on him for quality results. Therefore, he feels compelled to guard against his friends seeing him as inefficient or substandard. Owls are often driven to cover up their mistakes so they do not look incapable or inaccurate in the eyes of others.

Doves tell white lies for a different reason. They fear being seen as harsh, selfish, or unsympathetic. Thus, doves might stretch the truth to project kindness and thoughtfulness. You might hear them say, "That's a beautiful sweater you're wearing," even though they dislike it. Or "The dinner you made was delicious," despite the fact that they did not enjoy it. Doves tell white lies to protect the feelings of others. Ironically, doves value sincerity, but their white lies embody insincerity.

Parrots, who like to impress others, are known to embellish the truth. If a story is good but not great, they might embellish the facts to make it more exciting. Parrots like to project that everything works out well for them because their self-image is based on that reality. At the same time, they like to be seen as fun-loving optimists. So if something bad happens, they may describe the event as if it were an incredible adventure instead of a traumatic experience. Parrots like to be liked, and they may exaggerate the facts so they don't look bad and, therefore, become less likable.

The next time you judge others for telling white lies, consider that their style is driving their behavior. And remember, everyone tells white lies based on their personality style . . . even you.

The Chameleon Student

Our relationships are built on foundations of honesty, but as the birds learned in *Mudslide*, everybody lies in one way or another. We tell white lies to protect the feelings of others, and we exaggerate or twist the truth so as not to embarrass ourselves. Children lie so they don't get in trouble. Come to think of it, adults do that too.

People's opinions do not define you. How you see yourself defines you. Nonetheless, peer pressure and the overwhelming desire to make new friends and get good grades can cause us to lie.

Imagine a Dove whose roommate plays loud music while she is trying to study. The roommate has asked if the volume is too high, but the Dove doesn't want to offend her roommate. So, the Dove dismisses the loudness of the music as no big deal. Over time, the Dove becomes resentful yet resists sharing her true feelings. If the Dove had initially answered candidly, she might have avoided this conundrum.

When you are tempted to stretch the truth, consider the source of this temptation. As an Eagle, are you afraid to appear weak? As a Parrot, are you concerned that others won't see you in a positive light? Doves, do you worry that others won't like you or think you're unkind? And Owls, do you want to protect your reputation as someone who doesn't make mistakes?

The more we understand and accept ourselves, the less we feel a need to alter the truth. When we understand that mistakes are human, we don't need to mask our perceived imperfections. We embrace them instead. Vulnerability builds trust, credibility and accountability with others.

Hold onto your integrity. Be honest with friends, parents and instructors. You will like the version of yourself that speaks the truth.

- AVOID JUDGING OTHERS for telling white lies. We all tell them.

- NOTE THAT A WHITE LIE IS SERVING a deeper personality-driven need.

- CONSIDER THE IMPACT of being completely truthful and how that could positively impact the relationship.

- CONSIDER THE WHITE LIES YOU TELL and ask yourself whether your perceived negative impact of telling the truth is real or imagined.

- RECOGNIZE THAT THE BETTER you know and accept yourself, the more truthful you will become.

Winter Camp

Three days ago, winter camp had begun for the children of Home, and Simon and Ivory were ready for the challenge. The camp provided a place where little ones could go when their parents were taking a winter vacation. The adults took turns volunteering at the camp, and today Simon and Ivory were tasked with keeping the children safe and entertained.

The campers were usually excited to be together at camp, but on rainy days many of the fun activities were cancelled. When Simon arrived, he did not have a good feeling about the weather. The sun was nowhere to be seen, and the clouds threatened a torrential downpour. The dove worried that the children would not enjoy themselves with a rainy day activity schedule. He was also concerned about his ability to engage the campers because he was not accustomed to taking the lead.

By the time the children arrived, the cold winter rain was falling down hard. The youngsters gathered below an assemblage of large leaves that had been woven together to protect them. Twenty of the youngest looked at Simon excitedly, anticipating the fun that awaited them.

Simon hopped up on a branch and called everyone to attention. "Hello campers," he said invitingly. It took a few moments before the kids looked his way. "I'm sorry you won't be able to participate in your normal activities today, but the rain . . . Well, don't worry. We will make do."

Simon was not surprised to hear a loud groan emanate from the group. "I know. I know. I'm sorry. Since we are implementing the rain plan today, I need you to listen carefully so you all know what to do."

The campers let out another loud groan.

"Let's make the best of it everyone," the dove requested. "The first activity today is leaf origami."

"Are you kidding?" a young eagle complained.

"Seriously?" a young parrot squawked. "That's not going to be fun at all!"

One owl whispered to another, "He had weeks to create a rain plan, and all he could come up with is a game for babies?"

"Don't worry. It will be fun. Let's begin."

As the group begrudgingly played with their leaves, Simon heard Ivory and her campers, who were gathered nearby. Ivory had a loud parrot voice, and he could hear everything she was saying. She was running a little behind schedule and was only now announcing her group's first activity.

"Are you ready for some crazy rainy day fun?" Ivory called to her campers.

"Good luck with that," Simon reflected, as he picked up a leaf with the hope of turning it into the shape of a dragonfly.

A few of the oldest campers returned a halfhearted "yes" to Ivory.

The parrot repeated louder, "*I said*, are you ready for some crazy rainy day fun?!"

"YES!" the group returned.

"So who thinks they've got what it takes to be The Origami Champion?" Ivory challenged.

A loud "meeeeee!" echoed through the forest.

"I can't hear you," she replied. "Who here can make something awesome from their leaf? Something so cool that all the other leaves in the forest will be calling your name and asking you to fold them into something amazing?"

"Meeeeee!" shouted the chorus of campers.

Ivory hopped down from her branch and began weaving in and out of the members of her group. She lowered her voice as if she were sharing a great secret. "Here's what we are going to do. First, each of you will select a leaf from my Big Basket of Fun. Then, I'll be looking for the craziest, wackiest, funniest, silliest leaf you can muster. Who thinks they can win the Rainy Day Crazy Leaf Origami Challenge?"

Again, a loud choir of "meeeeee" reverberated throughout the land.

"Let's do it!!!" Ivory cheered. "Grab a leaf and let the games begin!"

Simon just shook his head. "I do not get it. My campers are doing the same thing as her campers, yet her kids are looking forward to it and mine are dreading it. How does she do that?"

"I think I can help," offered a quiet voice that resonated beside him. "Oh!" Simon jumped. "I didn't see you there Xenia and Xander. You startled me."

The pair emerged from beneath a large piece of foliage that was being propped up with two twigs. Xenia was holding a leaf that she had turned into a stunning replica of a chipmunk. The detail was astonishing, right down to its joyful facial expression. Xander held a leaf that looked as if it had been simply folded a few times.

Simon smiled politely at Xander as he held up his creation and said, "It's a turtle. See, here's the head. These are his feet. It's a turtle."

Xenia winked at Simon. "It seems like you've got a tough group of campers," the chameleon noted.

"Oh, I don't think so," conceded Simon. "I think it's me."

Xenia revealed the hint of smile. "It sounds like Ivory has everything under control."

"I know. That's what makes me think it's me," the dove said.

Xenia turned to her young student and asked, "Xander, what do you do when you're not sure how to handle a situation?"

"That's easy," Xander answered. "I just ask myself, 'What would Xenia do?'"

"Hum. That's interesting," Xenia replied.

"Well, the rain seems to be picking up. I need to get Xander home to his parents. You have a great day," Xenia said, as she and her protégé shifted their coloring to match the fertile-brown earth below them.

The noise from Ivory's campers drowned out the near silence of Simon's group. "That was an odd interaction," the dove thought. "Xenia usually helps me. But this time, she didn't say anything."

When it was time to introduce the next exercise, Simon was still thinking about what Xander had said, and that's when it struck him. Though he may not naturally *think* like a parrot, that doesn't mean he can't *act* like one for a little while. So Simon relaxed, closed his eyes and thought, "What would Ivory do?"

"I need to turn up my energy. If I am not having fun, they will not have fun. I need to get excited to get them excited. Well, here goes nothing."

The dove glanced down at his list and saw that his second activity was called Council Elder.

"Attention everyone," he called. "Can I have your attention, please?"

Simon knew that they preferred sunny day activities to rainy day ones, but he was on a mission to make this day fun. After a few more requests for silence, the group became quiet. He took a deep breath and thought, *Be like Ivory. That is all I have to do. Be like Ivory.*

With a burst of energy, Simon cheered, "Who thinks you can outsmart the rest of your fellow campers?"

A few wings tentatively raised into the air. "That's it?" he questioned. "Let us try that again." With even more energy, Simon added, "Who among you can out-think, out-logic, out-reason your fellow campers?"

This time, many of the campers lifted their wings into the air. He even noticed a few smiles as well.

"Very good, then," Simon commented. He pointed to Dean, a young eagle who seemed rather confident that he was up for the challenge. Simon directed the youngster to hide behind a nearby tree and then informed him that he would retrieve him soon and give him instructions.

Simon then turned to face the group, crouched down real low, and whispered, "Come closer everyone. I will tell you what we are going to do."

Simon selected one of the doves and instructed, "You are going to be the Council Elder. You are free to move however you like. The rest of us will repeat everything you do. If you smile, we will all smile. If you tap your foot, we will all tap our feet. If you stick out your tongue and try to touch the tip of your beak, we will all stick out our tongues."

Simon stuck out his tongue and crossed his eyes. Everyone laughed.

"Now, everyone else, in addition to following everything the dove does, you can also do anything you like, but nobody else will be copying you. When Dean returns, he has to figure out who the Council Elder is. Can you fake him out?"

"Yes," the group responded.

"I can't hear you," Simon said as he widened his eyes and placed his left wing beside his head.

"*Yesssss!*" returned the cheerful campers.

Dean returned and the group began laughing from start. Simon could not believe his eyes. He had done it. He had turned his unhappy campers into a joyful bunch of children.

Simon took out his pencil so that he would not forget what he just learned. "Whenever I need to do something that is not natural for me," he wrote, "identify someone who would do it well and ask myself what that individual would do . . . then do it."

Simon smiled as he looked at the day's third activity. He could already hear the laughter from Ivory's group and he was confident that he would make it fun for his campers as well . . . just like Ivory would do.

As Xenia and Xander secretly observed Simon from behind a tree, a large box turtle slowly walked by the chameleons. Xander thrust his origami art forward and said, "See, it's a turtle! It looks just like him."

Chameleon Wisdom

Act the part and you will become the part.
—WILLIAM JAMES

Throughout our lives there are times when our natural style is perfectly suited for the situation we are in. However, there are also occasions in which we need to display behaviors that are not typically associated with our innate approach to the world. Imagine a strong parrot speaking with a software Help Desk. The rep requests, "Tell me what's happening." The parrot replies, "I don't know. The thingy just stopped working."

This parrot is faced with the everyday experience of needing to tap into behaviors that are not natural.

In this situation, the parrot needed to be highly specific, despite his tendency to speak in generalities. The ability to flexibly display behaviors that are not native to our style is critical to our success. Yet, sometimes the required actions are so foreign to us that we have no idea what to do.

Fortunately, there are masters of each style, and they are all around us. They are our coworkers and our family members. They are on television, in books and movies, and scattered throughout human history. These experts are the people who strongly embody the characteristics of the bird styles.

The next time you get stuck and do not know what to do, ask yourself, "Who would be great at handling this situation?" Then imagine yourself acting like they would act. Visualize yourself adopting their body language, posture, facial expressions, wording, tone, and pace.

When we act as if we are a certain type of person, we can become that person, even if it is just for a little while. Holding the body language of someone we would like to emulate creates an emotional readiness to display the behaviors we want to exhibit.

As we watch someone display a behavior, or simply picture that action in our mind's eye, our brains activate the same neurons as if we were enacting that behavior ourselves. Amazingly, just thinking about a behavior creates the hardwiring for it. So when it comes time to engage in the action, it is easier for us to do so because our brains have been prewired.

In *Winter Camp*, Simon watched Ivory and replicated her behaviors. His positive self-talk empowered him to act like a parrot. When it came time to energize the kids, the dove became more animated and spoke with greater enthusiasm. He did not change who he was, but rather, for a short time *acted as if* he were a parrot.

As our inner voice tells us how to respond to challenges, our thoughts create our reality. When we imagine ourselves easily resolving difficult issues and then putting new behaviors into practice, we gain inner strength. Over time, we will be able to spontaneously display formerly uncomfortable behaviors and turn obstacles into opportunity.

Imagine an eagle who has to deal with a frustrated dove customer or, perhaps, an upset dove spouse. The natural tendency of an eagle is to charge forward and try to fix the problem. However, doves need emotional validation. They want to know that we understand and feel their pain. Only then, are they ready to look forward to a solution.

But this eagle does not know what to say or how to display empathy. In addition to directly asking how to act, the eagle has several viable options. First, the eagle could ask another dove what to do. If another dove is available, this a simple way to understand a dove's needs.

Second, the eagle could reflect back on how this particular dove has handled other upset people in the past. Since we treat others how we ourselves like to be treated, looking at how this dove has treated others in a similar situation provides a window into the dove's needs.

Third, the eagle has been presented with the opportunity to develop new hardwiring that can be used in this and similar occasions in the future. The eagle might identify a dove who would naturally handle this situation effectively. This could be a person that the eagle knows, a famous person, or a fictitious character. The eagle could visualize this individual responding to the dove, while paying attention to the body language and words that are employed.

With new hardwiring in place, the eagle can embody that person's energy and implement new actions. While these behaviors may not feel natural, the attempt is likely to yield better results than if the eagle responded in eagle mode. In fact, if the dove is the eagle's spouse, the eagle is likely to gain points for making an attempt to be empathetic.

As we engage new behaviors, we create a mental script that guides future actions. We stretch ourselves and gain comfort with a greater range of responses. And while these new behaviors may never become core strengths, at least they will not inhibit our effectiveness.

While *acting as if* can be scary, it can also be fun to approach problems with a new state of mind.

The Chameleon Student

How easy life would be if we were good at everything we tried! Of course, that's not reality. Some classes will be harder than others. Most sports will not be in our wheelhouse. Perhaps technology is not our friend.

In the world of personality, we all have strengths and we all have challenges. Some things feel so easy and natural, we can't imagine that others find them difficult. Other things feel so difficult and unnatural, we can't believe others find them easy.

We all have that Owl friend who in minutes diagnoses a computer problem we spent an hour trying to troubleshoot. We know that Parrot who schmoozes his way into the teacher's good graces and that Eagle who takes charge to change a project due date that the class finds unfair. And we all have that Dove friend who says just the right thing to cheer us up when we are down.

As the birds learned in *Winter Camp*, teachers are all around us. Everywhere we look, there are those who have mastered one or more of the four styles. They may not know they are masters, but living as an Eagle, Parrot, Dove or Owl makes them so. Most would be happy to teach you about their style.

You can study other people in action and think, "What would they do?" in your situation. Even better, ask the masters. What Eagle wouldn't be eager to tell you how to stand up for yourself if you felt cheated out of a higher grade? What Parrot wouldn't jump at the chance to talk you through how to energize the club you lead? What Dove wouldn't want to share how you can help a friend through a tough breakup with a long-term boyfriend or girlfriend? And what Owl wouldn't be willing to explain how to manage time and study during finals?

Don't be offended if the people you seek advice from say their recommendations are "easy" to follow. It's simple for them because they are hardwired for those actions. Know that you can lay down new hardwiring with repeated practice. Soon enough, behaviors you found challenging and uncomfortable will be a part of your repertoire.

- PAY ATTENTION TO OTHER PEOPLE who effortlessly act in ways that are challenging for you.

- COMMIT TO TRYING out new behaviors; eventually they will flow spontaneously.

- VISUALIZE YOURSELF AS THE PERSON you wish to emulate. Take on every aspect of their style and let go of inhibitions.

- LET GO OF HOW WELL YOU PERFORM when you try new behaviors.

- RECOGNIZE THAT acting as if you are someone else does not mean that you are trying to change who you are. Rather, you are simply doing what needs to be done in a situation because those behaviors are the ones that are needed.

The Northern Squirrels

When Simon awoke, a soft coating of snow mirrored the whiteness of his dove feathers. He always enjoyed the winter season, when crystal snowflakes made the forest sparkle. But this year was a challenging one for him and for many of the other forest dwellers. For the past few weeks, Simon and many of his dove friends and family members were having a hard time locating seeds. With each passing day, the birds grew more concerned about their winter stockpiles.

Simon headed out early to see if he could find some food to bring back to his loved ones, but he was having no luck. He searched the weeds and grasses where seeds were typically found, but the seeds—all of them—were gone. Someone had taken them. The dove stared helplessly at the snow-covered forest, wondering what to do next.

Dee, circling above the treetops, noticed her dove friend and approached to see what he was doing. Simon explained the lack of food and shared his fears about making it through the frosty winter. He worried especially about the youngest and oldest in the dove community. How could they survive the season without enough nourishment?

Dee looked at Simon curiously. "I just heard that the doves in the Northern Territory are having the same problem. I also heard that the squirrels up north are enjoying an abundance of food this winter."

"That's interesting," Simon commented. "For the past few weeks, I've seen lots of northern squirrels carrying food throughout the forest. You don't think the squirrels planned this, do you?" He shivered at the thought.

"I think it's clear what has happened. They took your food, and I'm going to help you fix it. Let's head north and ask the squirrels to return some of the food. If they are unwilling, we will take it."

"Whoa," Simon protested. "I am sure they will understand our situation. If we go there and express our concerns, certainly they will be willing to help."

"Help? What are you talking about? They took your food. Returning it isn't being helpful. It is doing what must be done," said Dee.

"I'm sure that they don't realize what they did," Simon responded. "If we just talk with them . . ."

"Okay. Let's get one thing straight. They know exactly what they did. You are not a bear who can sleep your way through winter, and neither are the other doves, who must be hungry by now. I'm thinking that you are going to want to eat sometime before spring."

They spoke for a few more minutes but found it hard to find common ground. In fact, the more they talked, the farther apart they became. Simon requested they spend the rest of the day thinking about each other's perspectives before actually doing anything. They planned to meet again the next morning to formulate a strategy.

Later that evening, as the chatter of the frogs gradually replaced the conversations of the birds, Simon sat alone looking out at the Great Lake. As the sky reflected the sunset's radiant red onto the pale ice, his dove feathers blended effortlessly into the dusting of snow decorating his branch.

Simon felt depleted from the day. However, what drained him most was not the content of their discussion, but rather, its tone. The dove was not thinking about the squirrels right now. Instead, he was reflecting on how Dee had communicated with him. While he appreciated her help, he felt as if Dee was condescending in her manner. "She didn't have to be so harsh," he thought. "I would never speak to someone like that."

As the snow continued to fall, Simon shook his head in frustration.

On the other side of the lake, Dee majestically gazed out over the great expanse of the wilderness. She, too, was thinking about her talk with Simon. *What a colossal waste of time that was*, she thought. *Simon is unwilling to take bold steps to fix the problem.*

Dee believed that they should have been able to solve this problem hours ago, but until now they hadn't settled a thing. Now they would have to continue the conversation when, instead, they should be investing their energy into fixing the problem. As Dee watched the snow blanket the forest, she knew the urgency of the situation was becoming more pronounced every day.

After a long, cold night, the dove and eagle met again in the morning. Dee arrived early, eager to resolve the issue. Simon arrived late. The dove was withdrawn and could barely make eye contact with the eagle.

Simon answered questions with one word answers such as "fine" and "whatever," which only irritated Dee even more. In turn, she became more blunt and aggressive, which further aggravated the situation.

That was it. Dee had had enough. "I don't see how we are going to figure this thing out with you acting like this."

Simon was stunned. "Me acting like what?" For the life of him, he couldn't figure out what she was talking about. He felt Dee's tone was getting in the way of finding a reasonable solution.

Dee could not believe what she was hearing. All she was trying to do was help, and Simon was getting in the way of progress. "This is crazy!" Dee snapped.

Simon sighed in frustration.

Just then, a puff of snow fell from the branch above them. They both looked up and noticed a white tail sliding down the trunk of the tree and heading towards them. "May I join you?" Xenia requested politely.

"Please do," Simon answered with relief.

"I guess so," Dee shrugged.

"I couldn't help but overhear your conversation. It sounds like you are at an impasse," the chameleon observed.

"You can say that again," the eagle snarled.

Lowering his head, Simon agreed.

"You are pushing each other's buttons and frustrating each other," the chameleon explained.

"I don't see how I am doing anything wrong," Dee proclaimed adamantly. "I am willing to do whatever it takes to fix the problem. A problem, I might add, that Simon asked me to help him solve.

I'm just being candid in expressing what we must do. Simon is avoiding the issues and isn't willing to take definitive action."

"And that bothers you?" Xenia asked.

"You're darn right!" the eagle declared.

The chameleon then turned to Simon. "And you're upset with Dee?"

"Well, yes, I am," the dove said hesitantly. "She's not being respectful."

"Talk with me," Xenia prompted. "Tell me more about how she is not being respectful."

Dee was about to snap back at Simon, but Xenia lifted her hand to stop her so that Simon could respond. "Simon, continue," she instructed.

"She's not listening, and she speaks to me in a harsh and pushy way. I don't want to seem ungrateful because I truly appreciate her help, but I would never treat her like that."

"So she is pushing your buttons, too?" Xenia asked.

"I guess so."

"It has been my experience that if someone is pushing my hot buttons, it is possible that I am also pushing theirs," Xenia advised.

Dee thought about that for a moment, and then replied. "So you're saying that every time someone is annoying me, I am probably annoying them, too?"

"Yes," Xenia acknowledged with a nod.

"Oh, that is not good," Dee chuckled. "If that's really the case, I must bother a lot of folks."

Simon and Xenia laughed as well.

"That makes sense," Simon acknowledged. "It upset me that Dee was being too blunt, and now I sense that I frustrated her because I was not being assertive enough."

"I'd agree with that," confirmed the eagle.

Xenia continued, "The fact that you push each other's buttons means that you have something to learn from each other."

The chameleon flicked her tail, shooting a wisp of snow into the air. Just before she leapt to an adjacent branch and disappeared into the snow, she whispered, "Those who bother us most can often teach us best."

Before they could thank the chameleon, she was gone.

"You do kinda push my buttons," Simon smiled.

"And you definitely push mine," Dee grinned. "But we've got work to do. How about this? Why don't we go talk to the northern squirrels? We'll start off with your plan. I won't say a word. But if they are not receptive to giving us back some food, I will become a little more assertive."

"Sounds good to me," Simon said. "But remember, they're not bears, either. They need to eat, too."

Chameleon Wisdom

If we learn to open our hearts, anyone, including the people who drive us crazy, can be our teacher.
—PEMA CHÖDRÖN

When two people enter each other's lives, each has something to gain from the other. While at times the relationship may seem lopsided, no two people come together to benefit just one of them.

Sometimes we come across people who we find difficult to deal with. Perhaps those closest to us have habits that annoy or confound us. These people are not in our lives to be conquered. They are there to be understood so we can better understand ourselves. In fact, our greatest teachers are often those who evoke deep emotional responses as they provide us with opportunities to learn.

While these teachers may generate stress or adversity, the situations they trigger help us to stretch ourselves and grow. So instead of blaming them for their shortcomings, thank them for providing the opportunity to practice tolerance and acceptance. Appreciate that they give us the chance to practice useful conflict management and negotiation skills that we will surely need in the future as we struggle to meet our own needs. These people help us see ourselves differently and, thus, increase our own self-awareness. And if we are feeling particularly open and gracious, we can thank them for reflecting our own issues back to us.

While it is hard to feel appreciative of someone who seems to be making our lives more difficult, try to look inside and understand the hot button they are pressing, instead of reacting with defensiveness or anger.

People push our buttons for many reasons. Sometimes individuals upset us because they are reflecting back to us our own shortcomings or the parts of ourselves we do not like. They may reflect fears, unresolved issues, or disliked behaviors that we subconsciously adopted from someone else. These people act like mirrors, revealing a part of ourselves that we try to hide from others. They can also reflect a former version of ourselves that we do not want to revert to.

Those individuals whose personalities and actions push our hot buttons are often our greatest teachers. They help us to see, to heal, and to gain balance. In *The Northern Squirrels*, Dee and Simon had different approaches to the squirrel problem. If they had been willing, Dee could have learned how to approach others with an open heart, while Simon could have learned how to be more assertive. Simon reflected Dee's impatience and insensitivity. Dee reflected Simon's inability to stand in his own power.

As Dee and Simon have taught us, when someone pushes our hot buttons, it is likely that we are pushing theirs. Imagine a parrot and owl couple who need to pick up a few things at the grocery store. The owl usually does the shopping, but, in this instance, the parrot is coming along. The owl, wanting only to help the parrot, provides concise directions on where items are located in the store. The owl draws a map and highlights the pathway that the parrot should follow. Instead of feeling appreciative, however, the parrot feels micromanaged and starts tuning out the owl's instructions. The owl has pushed one of the parrot's buttons. The owl then gets annoyed because the parrot is not listening, which means she will be more likely to be inefficient or forget something. The parrot has pushed one of the owl's buttons.

Our emotions are triggered when our desires are not met. When our core needs are not honored, we can get frustrated, angry, or resentful. And yet, in those times when we do not understand someone else, chances are, they do not understand us, either. In other words, you may be just as difficult a person in the eyes of the person you find difficult.

Consider two young eagle and owl siblings. To their parents' dismay, they are constantly bickering. The eagle annoys the owl because the eagle does not follow the rules. The pair agreed on specific shower times before school, but the eagle often stays in the shower too long. In addition, the eagle invites friends over while their parents are not home, which is a clear violation of their parents' rules. The owl resents that the eagle is breaking the rules while he is following them.

Meanwhile, the owl annoys the eagle because the owl is slow. One house rule is that the entire family must remain at the dinner table until everyone has finished eating. Each night, the owl takes much longer to complete his dinner, which frustrates the eagle, who eats much faster. The eagle is also bothered that the owl takes too long to finish his homework because another rule is that the house must remain quiet until everyone's homework is complete.

Both the eagle and the owl are annoying each other because their style-driven needs are not being met. Eagles move at a fast pace and are frustrated by slowness. Owls adhere to rules and are dismayed by those who view them as loose guidelines. While they are each having their own hot buttons pressed, they fail to realize that they are also pushing the other's buttons.

We are all here to help each other grow. Take a step back and accept that we push the buttons of the person who is pushing ours. This realization puts us on equal footing with the other person.

It is said that when the student is ready, the teacher will appear. We are all students and we are all teachers, each of us doing the best we can by being who we are. Along the way, we may push a few buttons and have a few of our own pushed, as well. But when we open ourselves to the gifts that others give us when they create adversity in our lives, we learn the lessons that we need to learn most.

The Chameleon Student

School exposes us to an array of Eagles, Parrots, Doves and Owls. If you haven't already encountered someone (or many someones) who push your buttons, you will. *And that's where the opportunity lies!* You'll learn how to navigate the rough waters of difficult relationships. You'll learn how to manage the inevitable conflict that arises. But most of all, you'll learn how to deal with characters who interact with people in a different way than you do.

As the birds discovered in *The Northern Squirrels*, if someone annoys you, your behaviors may bother that individual as well. Try to understand what it is about that person that troubles you. Does she resemble a more aggressive, insensitive 'version' of yourself that you worked hard to change? Does he bombard you with advice in situations where you feel it would be better to ask questions and listen? Do you feel jealous of someone who always delivers the funny one-liner before you can chime in? Conversely, how might your actions fuel the other person's feelings of irritation, misunderstanding or insecurity?

Style differences will arise in your daily life. The sloppy roommates and neat roommates eventually tangle. On big projects, the people who plan ahead may clash with those who wait until the last minute. The blunt teacher might seem to lack compassion, while the unstructured teacher might seem disorganized. Each encounter can teach you to accept people and deal with them more skillfully. The ability to accept others will serve you throughout life.

Drama is inevitable. Getting drawn into it is optional. Seek to understand the source of your annoyance. Try to find a way to get along with others and relinquish judgment. If you learn these skills now, you will spare yourself a lifetime of stress and conflict.

- RECOGNIZE THAT PEOPLE do not do things against you, but rather, for themselves.

- MANAGE YOUR EMOTIONS when dealing with button-pushers who are different from you.

- STOP TAKING THINGS PERSONALLY and gain control of your emotions.

- DO NOT TRY TO CHANGE OTHERS. Look inside and see which one of your thoughts needs to be adjusted.

- LET GO OF JUDGMENT and accept others for who they are.

Lost in Translation

After enduring a particularly relentless winter, Ivory was more than ready to escape the cold. Though it took significant prodding, she finally convinced her friends—Dee, Simon, and Carl—to head southeast for some sun and excitement.

The parrot agreed to map out the journey, while Carl took on the responsibility of coordinating their meals. Arranging four different diets in a foreign land would be no easy task, but the owl was up for the challenge.

Simon was a little worried because the residents of the Eastern Tidelands spoke a different language, but Dee's confidence assured the dove that everything would be alright.

The four companions met just after sunrise at the Council Tree. They hoped to get an early start on their adventure. As they leaped into the blue unknown, Ivory knew exactly where she was headed—the Eastern Tidelands.

They were supposed to follow the river to the Crystal Cave and then to the edge of Home. From there, she was certain she could figure it out. After all, many of Home's residents visited this popular vacation spot, and they always found their way. *How hard can it be to get there*, Ivory thought.

A few hours into the journey, Dee asked, "How are we doing with time?"

"Great!" Ivory proclaimed. "We're right on track."

"Excellent," the eagle replied.

"And you're positive that we are on the right path?" Carl questioned.

"We're always on the right path," Ivory affirmed. This didn't completely satisfy the owl, but it would have to do for now.

When they stopped to eat, Carl removed four individually-packed meals from his satchel. In preparation for the trip, he had carefully selected some of his friends' favorite meals. For Simon, a beautiful array of nuts, including his beloved sunflower seeds. For Ivory, an assortment of fresh fruit, including her favorite, star fruit. For Dee and himself, well, let's just say there are fewer chipmunks in the forest.

A few hours later, Ivory informed the group that it was time to make camp for the evening. "This looks like as good a place as any to tuck in for the night."

When they awoke, they enjoyed another thoughtful meal prepared by Carl before they continued onward. To Ivory's delight, they arrived a few hours later, just minutes after the time she had expected to arrive. Ivory was eager to get closer to the water. She had never seen giant waves like these before. They were huge compared to the waves she and Dee had seen at a smaller beach last summer.

The four friends stood on the hot sand and listened to the beautiful seaside sounds. They were fascinated by the hypnotic rumbling of the waves rolling out to sea and back again with mighty crashes. The peculiar squeals of seagulls filled the air above them. The forest had no seagulls, so the four friends couldn't understand a word the seagulls were saying. It simply sounded like pure chatter, without any meaning.

The friends stood for quite a while, enjoying the salty air and listening to the unfamiliar sounds. They were delighted to see a pod of dolphins swimming near the shore and to hear their distinctive clicks and squeaks. They wished they understood dolphin dialogue. After a while, a pair of owls flew by and landed on a nearby palm tree. Even with noisy seagulls squawking all around them, the friends were able to tune in and understand the owls' conversation about the rhythmic timing of the waves.

The friends spent the next few days thoroughly enjoying their adventure away from Home. They tried unusual foods, slept in new kinds of trees, and even attempted surfing on strips of palm bark. By the time they were ready to leave, three of the friends were quite good at surfing. Simon chose not to try. He preferred to encourage the others from the safety of the beach. Simon enjoyed building sand castles and writing words of encouragement in the sand, such as "Way to go!" His words lasted most of the day, until the tide finally came in and washed them away.

When they got home, the four friends were famished. They had opted to skip one of Carl's planned rest breaks so they could return by sundown. They decided to share one last meal together before returning to their respective trees.

After setting out the final vacation dinner, Carl noted, "I want to thank Ivory for making this trip happen. When she first approached me, I was a bit hesitant. But Ivory did a wonderful job of organizing the experience. She looked at maps and plotted our course. She timed out the trip with precision. She did a great job coordinating where we were going to sleep each night. Ivory, you are quite an efficient event planner."

"Actually," Ivory shrugged, "I just figured if we headed mostly southeast we'd eventually run into it. And we really lucked out finding good places to stay. I wasn't quite sure how that would work out, but I liked where we made camp. I love it when a plan comes together!"

"Hold on a moment," the owl stated. "Are you telling me that you didn't map out the . . ."

"Oh, don't worry about it, Carl. We made it, didn't we?"

"Yes, but . . ." Carl began.

"Great!" Ivory interjected. "Carl, did you enjoy the trip?"

"Of course I enjoyed it," the owl replied. "That's what I just said."

The parrot raised an eyebrow, "You did?"

"Of course. I was just telling you what a great job you did and how well-planned it was."

"Well, thanks then," the parrot said hesitantly. "And I absolutely loved what I ate. Everything was delicious. In fact, I had some of the best meals I've ever eaten. You're the man!"

"Uh, thanks, I suppose," Carl uttered.

"What do you mean by 'I suppose'? The food totally rocked!"

"Specifically, what did you like about it? Just in case I am arranging meals for you again, I'd like to know exactly what you liked and didn't like. Is there anything you would do differently?"

"All of it was fantastic! I'm not sure what you mean," Ivory said.

Carl needed greater clarification. "Not to sound ungrateful, but how am I supposed to replicate the success of selecting the meals without knowing exactly what you found so enjoyable?"

Xenia and Xander were watching the entire conversation from a nearby branch. Xenia whispered to her apprentice, "Xander, this is the moment you've been waiting for. I know you are ready. Do you feel you are?"

"I am," he whispered confidently.

"Okay," Xenia said. "When you appear to the birds, you do not have to cautiously edge yourself into the conversation from afar. Get as close as you can, and when they least expect it, *bam*! Pop in with your greeting."

"Got it," Xander smiled.

"Hey, we have to have some fun, too," laughed the teacher. "I'll wait over here. This one is all yours."

As Xander turned to make his way toward the birds, Xenia whispered from a short distance away, "Remember, don't share too much."

With a single nod, the young chameleon made his way to his first assignment. Nobody saw him coming, so he nestled in right between Simon and Dee. With his arms wide open, he announced, "Good evening, everyone!"

All four of them swiveled their heads around in surprise. Simon put his wing on his chest to catch his breath. Dee looked as if she were about to pounce.

"Welcome," Ivory said, while Dee took on a more relaxed posture.

"Thank you," Xander replied. "I couldn't help but overhear your conversation. It sounds like both of you did a great job in planning the trip."

"They did," Simon agreed.

"It also sounds as if you are each saying that you appreciate each other's work in making the trip happen, but your appreciation is not registering," the young chameleon offered.

"Ya know, he's right," Dee stated. "I like this chameleon."

The eagle turned to Xander and asked, "What else can you tell us?"

Xander continued. "Xenia recently taught me that when we compliment someone, we need to think about who we are praising. Otherwise, it's as if we are speaking a foreign language that makes no sense to them."

"So you're saying my feedback to Carl didn't even count?" Ivory asked.

"Interesting question," Xander answered. "I need to get going, but you might wish to ask Carl that."

All eyes turned to the owl. "I didn't get any feedback. I just heard that Ivory liked the food. I do not mean to sound unappreciative, but that does not help me."

"Help you? I couldn't have been more enthusiastic," Ivory exclaimed.

"I think that's the point," Carl replied. "I do not need energetic praise. I want the details."

"But how do the details inspire you? Details don't make you feel good."

"Feedback isn't meant to inspire," the owl explained. "It is meant to drive future behavior."

"Well, for future reference, if you gave me upbeat encouragement like I just gave you, I'd put it on a repeating loop for the whole flight home."

"But how does that serve you?" the owl puzzled. "You will not be able to improve next time without receiving specifics from this time."

Simon softly inserted himself into the conversation. "I think what we're discovering here is that praise must match the needs of the individual who is getting it or it doesn't register as feedback."

Ivory and Carl understood.

Dee, watching the conversation from the sidelines, added, "This reminds me of when we were on the Eastern Tidelands and the seagulls were speaking a different language. Then the pair of owls appeared. The owls spoke our language, so I was able to tune in to what they were saying. I felt like I was eavesdropping, but I couldn't help but listen."

"Exactly," Simon confirmed. "When those around us speak our language, we pay attention. When they do not, we don't even hear them."

Ivory cleared her throat. "So, Carl, I want to tell you that I found your selection of food to be flawless. I specifically appreciate that you considered each of our dietary restrictions. You selected the right meal for each time of day, and each of the meals was well-suited for what we were doing. You prepared light meals for our travels and more substantial meals in the evening. I personally liked the selection of entrées you chose for me. I enjoyed every one of them and wouldn't change a thing."

"Why, thank you," Carl smiled. "And your mapping out of the trip totally rocked! I had a blast!"

"Excellent!" Ivory grinned. "Ya know, I'm not 100 percent sure you mean that, but it feels good anyway. I'll be hearing that over and over in my head as I fly home."

They all laughed as they reminisced about their adventure and wondered where their next joint vacation would take them.

The young apprentice returned to his wise master. "Nicely done," Xenia praised. "I have one suggestion for you, however. It is best not to sneak up on eagles," she smirked.

"Now you tell me," Xander smiled. His heart raced as he glanced back at Dee.

Chameleon Wisdom

We believe we do a better job at giving feedback than we really do.
—RICK MAURER

Here are two universal truths: We all need feedback. And we do not get enough.

Most of us fail to give as much feedback as we ourselves desire, despite its many benefits and the fact that it costs absolutely nothing. Feedback helps us grow. It reinforces our self-esteem and makes us feel good. The most basic psychological principle tells us that behaviors that are rewarded tend to be repeated.

In the workplace, positive feedback can enhance our sense of achievement, increase motivation, heighten accountability, and lead to greater results. Yet workers regularly cite lack of feedback and recognition as one of their biggest complaints. It is one of the primary reasons people leave organizations.

In our personal relationships, positive feedback builds trust and strengthens connections. Expressing a positive sentiment toward another offers us the opportunity to show our appreciation for their valued contributions and greatest gifts.

When we receive positive feedback, the reward center in our brain becomes stimulated. So whether we are at home or in the workplace, positive feedback creates feelings of being valued and appreciated. This boosts our self-esteem and leaves us open to new and greater possibilities.

Even though positive feedback offers us many benefits, people still do not seem to provide that much of it. Or do they? We may be receiving more feedback than we realize, but since it is given in the wrong style, it does not trigger our hardwiring. As a result, it is discounted, or it does not register as feedback at all.

The standard advice for providing positive feedback does not take personality style into account. Experts typically suggest that positive feedback should be specific, timely, encouraging, sincere, impactful, and regular. It is hard to argue with that advice. However, the true power of positive feedback occurs when people receive praise that triggers their natural hardwiring.

In *Lost in Translation*, the birds screened out the sounds of the seagulls who spoke a different language. But when the owls were nearby, the birds became attentive and tuned in to every word. The owls spoke the language of the forest birds, and they listened. This is exactly how it works with feedback. We tune in to feedback provided in our language—our style. Conversely, we tune out feedback that is offered in a different style, despite its good intentions.

The most effective feedback is tailored to the recipient; it resonates with what is important to that person. Consider each of the four bird styles. *Eagles* value bottom-line results. Therefore, when providing feedback to eagles, focus on what they have accomplished and the impact they have had. Say something like, "You helped us achieve our objective. That allowed us to increase *this* or decrease *that*. Thank you."

Parrots are motivated by enthusiastic praise. Turn up the volume when praising them. Tell them, "You were fantastic! When you *did this*, you really exceeded my expectations. I totally appreciate everything you did! Great effort and enthusiasm. Thank you so much!"

Contrary to the parrots, *owls* need details. They want to know exactly what they did right and what they can improve next time. Take the time to walk through their project from beginning to end. Be certain to highlight specifics. Your attention to detail will show them that you truly understand the quality of their work.

Doves value genuine and sincere appreciation. They want to know that they made a difference for their coworkers and the people they serve. Share with them, "You truly impacted all of us in a positive way. I appreciate everything you have done. Your role in this project allowed us to support our customers, and I want to thank you for your hard work and dedication."

Imagine giving an eagle feedback as if she were an owl. Or giving an owl feedback as if he were a dove. The words and effort are likely to fall on deaf ears. We all need feedback, but it needs to be given in the right style. Praise given in the wrong language is like white noise. We hear it, but it has no value or meaning.

Be the person who makes someone else's day by providing the recognition they so deeply crave, and personalize the feedback so they receive the full power of the message.

The Chameleon Student

School activities offer invaluable opportunities to practice leadership, a skill that will serve you throughout your career. As a club officer or team captain, you may have to manage projects and people, delegate work and provide feedback. Most people in the working world will tell you that their leaders *don't* provide enough feedback or recognize and acknowledge their successes.

As the birds learned in *Lost in Translation*, feedback should match the style of the recipient. People often discount the feedback they receive and sometimes, they don't even consider it "feedback" at all because it didn't trigger their innate hardwiring.

Imagine a fellow project team member, an Owl, who delivers your presentation with passion and enthusiasm. You know the Owl stepped out of her comfort zone to turn up the energy. Reward this behavior with positive feedback. You can boost the Owl's self-esteem, and she will appreciate that you recognized her achievement.

Remember to provide feedback in the style of the recipient. Focus on the results and impact for the Eagle. Be enthusiastic for the Parrot. Provide details for the Owl and be sincere for the Dove. Note how elated people feel when you give feedback in their style.

In the working world, people want a manager who honors their contributions and helps them to develop their abilities. Learn the art of giving feedback, and you will become a revered leader.

- DON'T LET GOOD WORK GO unnoticed.

- RECOGNIZE THAT ONE-SIZE-FITS-ALL feedback does not work.

- CONSIDER THE STYLE OF THE PERSON to whom you are giving feedback, and provide it to them the way they like it, not the way you like it.

- ACTIVELY LOOK FOR PEOPLE DOING THINGS WELL, then tell them! You may be surprised how many great things you discover.

The Magic Rock

Ivory and Carl watched the sun trace its familiar path across the morning sky. Ivory had found some snow-frozen blueberries, and she shared them with her owl friend. The parrot loved how the berries burst with sweetness in her mouth, as if each one had a joyful surprise in its center. Soon their conversation wound its way to comments about Xenia, their teacher and mentor. They talked about how much the chameleon had helped them over the years and decided to thank her for the impact she had made on their lives. Xenia had a special way of appearing exactly when her friends needed her most, and the pair wanted to give her a gift of appreciation. Now they had to figure out what that would be.

Together they ran through options, but nothing seemed quite right. A caricature drawing of Ivory, Carl, Dee, and Simon from their trip to the Eastern Tidelands? A box of maple-smoked crickets? A framed quotation from Xanadu? They rejected one idea after another until Carl remembered a story that Xenia had shared with them earlier in the year. The chameleon had described an egg-shaped rock that could be found only in the Crystal Cave. She talked about its "magic" powers.

"That's it!" Ivory declared.

"That's what?" Carl asked.

"Let's go to the Crystal Cave, find an egg-shaped rock, and bring it back to her as a gift."

"The cave is far and there's no guarantee we will find it. The unknown variables lower the probability of us locating an egg-shaped rock," the owl hypothesized. "We do not know how big it is, what it looks like, or even where to look once we get there."

"I'm sure we'll find one," the parrot affirmed. "She said they're in the cave."

After some careful consideration, and some prodding by Ivory, Carl reluctantly agreed.

"We will need to prepare for the trip," Carl advised. "We have to consider the tools that we will need to locate the rock and how we will transport it back here. Plus, it will take us a good part of the day to get there, so we need to determine how long the journey will take so we can figure out how much time we can spend at the cave. I would like to make it back before dark."

Ivory said, "It's really not a big deal. Even if we have to stay overnight, we will be home before the sun reaches the midday sky. And I know lots of folks who have traveled to the Crystal Cave for the day and made it back while it was still light. Trust me, we'll be fine."

"So when do you want to go?" Carl asked.

"No better time than the present. Let's go now!"

Given that Ivory knew many others who had traveled to the Crystal Cave and returned in a single day, Carl agreed to leave right away.

They flew past the Great Lake and followed the river as it twisted its way through the forest. After several hours of flying,

Carl grew concerned that the cave was still quite a distance away. The sun had passed the overhead position a few hours ago.

"Don't worry," Ivory reassured him. "It's not far at all. In fact, I believe it's just over these hills."

Carl breathed a sigh of relief. According to his calculations, if they arrived at the cave within the next few minutes, they would have about two hours to explore, find an egg-shaped rock, and make it back before it got dark.

After traveling for another half hour or so, Carl caught sight of a familiar rock formation. He was simultaneously comforted and annoyed. "Ivory," Carl said sternly. "Do you know where we are?"

"Yup. We're almost there," the parrot smiled knowingly.

"Actually, I recognize those rocks from our trip to the Eastern Tidelands. We are still about an hour away."

"That's what I said. We're almost there."

"In what forest does 'almost there' equal an hour?" the owl queried.

"Uh . . . this one?" Ivory stammered.

Carl was flabbergasted. "I trusted you. You told me you knew where we were going. You told me that this would be a day-trip!"

"Well, I'm mostly right," Ivory suggested. "We will get there today, and we'll have time to look for the rock. We just won't have time to get back by dark. That's pretty close to a win—especially if we find the magic rock."

"I don't want to argue. Let's just get there and find what we are looking for," Carl sighed.

"Hasn't that been the plan all along?" Ivory wondered.

After an hour of flying in silence, the pair followed the winding river to the cave. When they arrived, Ivory was concerned. "I've been in that cave before, and I've never seen a rock that looked like an egg. I think you should try to find it."

Just before Carl headed to the falls, Ivory advised, "Make sure you hit the water right beside that jutting rock." She pointed to a stone protruding from the cliff wall. "If you don't enter at exactly the right spot, you'll slam into a really hard rock," she advised, as she rubbed the top of her head in recollection.

"Got it," Carl replied before he took what felt like a leap of faith. The owl headed precisely where Ivory had instructed. After passing through the ice cold water, he found himself inside the cave. He could not believe his eyes. All around him were shimmering crystals of diverse and spectacular colors and sizes, just like the ones he had seen when he and Simon had watched Ivory create a mandala a few months earlier.

In the meantime, Ivory pushed aside underbrush, checked under stones, and inspected tall grass. She lifted smaller rocks to see if they were hiding anything beneath. All she yielded was a treasure trove of beetles and one very startled snake.

With the owl's ability to see in near darkness, Carl headed deeper into a long tunnel. He saw many rocks, and some sharp looking spikes that hung like cones from the ceiling or grew up from the ground like beams. The owl spotted stones that were long and flat, sharp and pointy, and round and irregular. But he didn't find anything that was remotely egg-shaped.

Carl had nearly given up when he decided to forge onward through a bend in the cave where he suspected few had ventured before him. As he picked up some long, flat slabs of rock, something caught his eye. The brown and muddy tip of a rock stuck out like a dome. He used his claws to wipe away the dirt and discovered a rock shaped like an egg, just as Xenia described it. When he tried to pick it up, he realized it was too heavy for him to move by himself. He called Ivory to provide assistance, and when she arrived, she found Carl staring at the ground.

The parrot had a difficult time seeing in the near darkness, so she bent down to feel the stone. "This is great!" Ivory proclaimed. "We found it!"

"Yes, we found it," Carl confirmed, "but now we need to get it out of here."

They tried lifting it but it was too heavy. Instead, they decided to roll the stone out of the cave so they could look at it in the sunlight. As they rolled the stone across the cave floor, Carl and Ivory got muddier and muddier. Pushing an egg-shaped rock through a cave was hard work for the two birds, and they knew they couldn't roll it all the way home.

Ivory washed the stone with water from the pool at the bottom of the falls, then she and Carl rinsed themselves off in the cool waters.

"This is it?" Carl asked. "It doesn't look like anything special."

Ivory smiled as she shook her body to dry herself. "Xenia said that the magic is inside."

The pair stood quietly staring at the rock as they tried to figure out how to get it home. Ivory broke the silence. "There is no way we are going to leave this thing here. There's gotta be a way to take it with us."

"I understand your desire to give this rock to Xenia, but we need to think this through."

"How about we just take turns carrying it?" Ivory suggested.

"That would be fine, but neither of us can lift it by ourselves," Carl replied. "We need to do this together."

"Okay. How about we grab hold of it and carry it as a team?"

"That does fix the carrying it alone problem, but we won't be able to fly like that," Carl stated.

"Maybe we need to get a flying start and grab it at full speed."

"Here, watch!" Ivory announced confidently.

Ivory backed up and gave herself some room to reach maximum velocity. As she rocketed towards the stone, Carl watched with a disapproving stare. To Ivory's credit, she managed to move the stone—about a stone's length from where it originally sat. She then tumbled in a whirlwind of precious reds, blues, and greens. When she came to a stop, she shook her head and said, "Well, now we know one way that *won't* work!"

The two gazed blankly at the egg-shaped rock for another minute until Ivory offered, "How about we tie a vine around it and we each hold one end of the vine? That oughta do it."

"Nope. That won't work either," Carl replied. "It will just slip out."

"Carl, all you do is cut down my ideas. You're like an idea beaver!"

"I have not yet heard a suggestion that will work. When I hear one, I will be quite complimentary."

"So what do you recommend, oh wise one?" Ivory sniped.

"Let's take this problem apart. One of us can't carry the rock alone. Yet to carry it together, we need to be some distance apart so that we can spread our wings. Utilizing vines sounds appealing, though the rock can slip out." Carl's eyes suddenly got big with inspiration. "How about we wrap the rock in large leaves and then tie long vines around the leaves? That will ensure that the rock stays secure, and it will give us the space to fly. This method will double our lifting power. And if we grab the vines after we already have some speed, the momentum will help us get it off the ground."

Ivory shook her head in disbelief. "So, basically, you've added a few leaves to all of my ideas, and now you want me to celebrate your brilliance?" the parrot protested.

"I am not looking for a celebration. I am looking for a methodology that works," replied the owl.

"You were clearly intent on cutting down all of my ideas, and then you go ahead and use them," Ivory huffed.

"That is not it at all. I was simply seeking a solution. Your ideas were not fully formed. Between the two of us, we have created a workable plan."

"Is that your way of giving me credit?" Ivory said.

"Let me get this straight. You spent an entire day misleading me, and now you want me to revel in your genius?"

"What are you talking about?" Ivory asked. "I didn't mislead you."

"From the beginning of our trip, you continually deceived me about how long it would take to get here. I would never have come today if I knew the real facts about this trip."

"I didn't lie," Ivory snapped defensively. "I believed we could make it."

"You must have said, 'We are almost there' a dozen times," the owl said.

"I wasn't lying. I was being optimistic. If I were to fly here thinking that we might get lost or not find the rock or not be able to make it back today, I would have been discouraged the entire way here. What's the point of that? My intention was simply to be positive."

"You didn't just hold positive thoughts," Carl complained. "You deceived me with your false optimism, and I made decisions on faulty data."

"I like to think positive thoughts, and I like to share what I think," Ivory said.

"But you had no facts to support your belief. I trusted you, and now we are not going to make it home tonight."

After a few more minutes of bickering, they decided to put their differences aside and attempt to carry the rock out of there. Carl wanted to cover as much distance as possible before it got dark so they wouldn't have as far to travel the next day. So off they went, once again, flying in silence as they carried the rock.

Flying with the extra weight was difficult, but neither one complained. When it became too dark to fly any farther, they agreed to make camp for the evening. Their muscles ached, but both birds sulked privately. Ivory made an occasional moaning sound as she cleared a place to sleep.

The next morning, they got up early with a goal of reaching home by noon. The long, quiet flight seemed to take forever.

When they finally got back, they had one last task to complete together. The pair arranged a dinner with some close friends for the next night. Xenia would be the guest of honor, and they would present her with the egg-shaped rock to thank her for sharing all of her wisdom. Ivory wrapped the stone in a beautiful array of flowers, and she and Carl were excited to present it to their chameleon teacher.

At the celebration, Dee and Simon sat between their owl and parrot friends. Simon could sense that something was wrong, but he didn't want to address the issue during this special evening. When Xenia arrived, she was escorted by Xander, who managed to get her there without revealing the true purpose of the event. After welcoming the chameleons to the festivities, Carl retrieved his Hatching Day Hat of Honor from beneath the table and presented it to Xenia. It didn't quite fit her, though she appreciated the sentiment. And Carl was happy to get rid of it.

After a delicious dinner, many of the guests spoke about Xenia and gave examples of how she often abruptly appeared out of nowhere and scared the living begeebers out of them. They talked about the many lessons she had taught them and thanked her for improving their lives.

After listening to the many tales told about the master chameleon, it was time to unveil their gift. With a great flourish, Ivory and Carl lifted the present into the air and spun it around so everyone could see it. Together, they placed it in front of their teacher, friend, and mentor.

Xenia was overwhelmed. While she gently removed the flowers and carefully placed them beside the stone, she thanked everyone for their kind words. After the rock was fully revealed, she slowly rolled it forward and backward with a beaming smile.

"This is one of my favorite wonders in the forest," she told the group. "Inside this stone are beautiful crystals that hold a secret message."

"What's the message?" Ivory shouted.

"I'm glad you asked," Xenia said with a grin. "The message is that we only see what's on the outside and make assumptions about what's on the inside. When you look at this rock and its dull brown-and-gray shell, you might assume that it is nothing special. *So what?* you might wonder. It's a brown-and-gray stone. But I can assure you there is much more to this rock on the inside. It is filled with sparkling crystals, and the only way to know what it looks like inside is to crack it open."

The group promptly gathered around the magical rock. Calls to crack it open rang throughout the group.

Xenia smiled and informed everyone that she would be right back. When she returned, she held a strange looking device she called "The Revealer." She walked over to the stone, glanced at Carl and Ivory, and said, "This reminds me of an important lesson."

Everyone cheered. After all, Xenia was being honored today for having shared so many lessons to those in attendance. The chameleon grinned and said, "Come now. You didn't expect to invite a chameleon to a gathering and not share a lesson, did you?"

"We were hoping you would," Ivory bantered, almost daring her to share just one more nugget of wisdom with all of them.

The group cheered even louder this time. When the chameleon turned her gaze to the stone, a hush fell over the forest. "Look at this amazing rock," she began. "You don't know what's inside. You only know what you see. But if you dig a little deeper, you may be surprised by the beauty you discover."

Everyone hung on her every word. Since she rarely had an opportunity to speak with so many of her followers at one time, she decided to delve a bit deeper. "And so it is with all of you. We see what's on the outside. We see what others do, but we do not know why they do it. In other words, we see actions but not intentions."

Xenia glanced at Carl and said, "Let me give you an example. For some, optimism creates the belief that everything will just work out. These folks tend to make gut decisions and truly believe everything will be okay. For others, decisions are better made based on data and analysis. For the more fact-based among us, optimism can be perceived as unrealistic. And when this optimism is imposed on others, it might even be interpreted as misguided or deceptive."

Carl understood. He was looking at Ivory's behavior as misleading, but really, Ivory was just being hopeful, which is not a bad thing.

Ivory felt vindicated. She knew she was not trying to trick Carl, but he judged her behavior to be deceptive.

Xenia then turned her attention to the parrot and asked, "Would another example be helpful?"

"Uh, sure," the parrot replied, secretly wishing that one example would be sufficient.

"Excellent," smiled Xenia with a subtle wink that only Ivory caught. "Sometimes, when others shoot down ideas, it's not because they are being critical of you. It's because they are analyzing the facts in order to make the right decision. For them, until the problem is completely resolved, there is no cause for celebration."

Ivory understood now that Carl was not being critical. He really just wanted a workable solution.

Xenia lifted The Revealer high into the air above the rock and offered one last piece of advice, "We judge ourselves based on intention, but we judge others based on behavior. Don't just look at what's on the outside. Consider what's on the inside as well. When you understand someone's style, you can determine their intention. And when you do, you shatter all judgment and discover the radiant center that lies at the core of each of us."

Xenia slowly and carefully positioned the device around the egg-shaped stone and, with a mighty crunch, split it in half to reveal . . .

Chameleon Wisdom

We judge ourselves by our intentions and others by their impact.
—JOHN WALLEN

We are well aware of our own intentions. We understand what motivates us. We are familiar with our deepest fears, hopes, and desires. When things do not go as we have planned or goals are not achieved, we cut ourselves some slack because we judge ourselves on our intention.

We have no access to the intentions others, and, accordingly, do not afford them the same leniency. We only know what we see. Therefore, we judge others based on their observable behaviors and results.

When we wish to gain a deeper understanding of why people behave as they do, we look to the only intentions that we are sure of—*our own.* Subconsciously, we superimpose our intentions on others by looking to what *our* intentions would be if we acted as they did.

Consider a dove watching an eagle confidently and vehemently make her point during a staff meeting. The dove perceives that the issue must be very important to the eagle. The dove knew that he, himself, would only have displayed that level of intensity if it were an issue of utmost importance to him. The dove judged the eagle's behavior based on what would prompt him, as a dove, to act in such an assertive manner. When it came time to make a decision, the dove backed down. The eagle's passion convinced him that the eagle must be right. He assumed the issue was critical to the eagle, and the dove did not want to deny her something of such importance to her. In reality, the eagle was simply expressing her views and had little attachment to her ideas or the issue.

In this scenario, the dove filtered the eagle's actions through the lens of his own intentions. This created an inaccurate interpretation of the eagle's needs and perspective. This demonstrates that we have it backwards. When it comes to ourselves, we should look at what we *do* rather than what we *intend*. For others, instead of considering only behaviors, we should look to what drives particular actions.

Making a shift to consider the intentions of others does not mean we should dismiss dysfunctional behaviors because someone "meant well." Positive intentions should not be used to justify disrespect, poor quality, or failed results. Harmful behaviors should be addressed and people should be held accountable for their actions, in spite of their intentions.

An owl cannot excuse his inability to meet a deadline with the justification that she wanted the project to be perfect before submitting it. Nor can a parrot excuse ignoring critical facts because he likes to make gut decisions based on intuition. Intention should not be used as an excuse.

While brainstorming solutions in *The Magic Rock*, Ivory and Carl each had positive intentions that negatively impacted the other. If they had considered each other's intentions, their conflict would have been minimized—or even avoided.

By understanding each other's internal motivators, we can look more accurately at the intentions of others. Consider what motivates parrots and owls. *Parrots* are energized by interacting with others. They desire freedom of expression, and they capitalize on opportunities to experience all that life has to offer. They are social, outgoing, and optimistic, and they thirst for adventure. When trying to interpret a parrot's actions, recognize that parrots are guided by the intention to enjoy life, not to avoid responsibility.

Owls seek precision, logic, structure, and clarity. They may ask a lot of questions, but do not take this as a sign of mistrust. They simply intend to do things right the first time. They will take every possible step to ensure quality outcomes. For the owl, if it is not going to be done right, then why do it? Understand that the intention behind the owl's behavior is to ensure reliable, consistent, and accurate results.

Imagine a parrot and owl couple on their day off from work. The parrot wants to have fun and then deal with their chores. The owl would prefer to complete their responsibilities first and then relax. The parrot needs to appreciate that the owl's thinking does not mean he does not intend to have fun. He just wants to finish the work first so it does not weigh him down. Conversely, the owl needs to grasp that it is not the parrot's intention to shirk responsibility. Rather, the parrot lives in the moment and wants to have fun for as long as she can before having to carry out chores.

Now consider what motivates eagles and doves. *Eagles* value autonomy, power, action, and candor. They are driven by an intention to get results, and they push back when something interferes with the achievement of their objectives. Eagles can be blunt and direct if they believe something is getting in the way of their productivity. Their intention is simply to achieve their goal.

Doves crave harmony, stability, comfort, and loyalty. They actively seek to minimize conflict, establish collaboration, and ensure trust and emotional safety. This may cause them to avoid confrontation or ignore glaring issues. Doves simply want everyone to get along. Their intentions are often infused with their need for peace and sensitivity.

Picture an eagle and dove couple. The eagle candidly points out the flaws in their child's school project, while the dove offers unconditional positive support. The eagle is irritated by the dove's lack of honesty, and the dove is offended by the eagle's forthrightness. By understanding the intentions behind their actions, the eagle and the dove can shift from judging each other's behaviors to valuing each other's contributions.

We prefer to be judged by intentions rather than actions or outcomes because we perceive our intentions to be well-meaning. Perhaps it is time to offer that same courtesy to others.

The Chameleon Student

As the birds experienced in *The Magic Rock*, we judge ourselves based on intention, but we judge others based on behavior. Imagine what would happen to conflict if we examined the intentions of others. Think about your parents. They may not act in ways that resonate with your style, but presumably they act in what they believe is your best interest.

Imagine how different parents might express good intentions during move-in week at college. What you perceive as indifference may be an Eagle parent's way of letting you take charge and feel independent. Your Parrot father might seem 'embarrassing' when he chats up all your dorm neighbors, hoping to introduce you to new friends. The Owl mom might seem overly critical about the classes you choose, while her goal is really to help you make good decisions. A week later, the daily phone calls from your Dove parent may feel smothering, even if they come from a place of love and support. Underneath it all, parents have your best interests at heart – though it may not always feel that way.

Likewise, when teachers assign a lot of work over a holiday weekend, their intent probably isn't to be mean or indifferent. They may be trying to cover required material that you'll need to know for an AP exam or MCAT. Perhaps they don't want to slam you with homework when midterms begin two weeks later.

Although we only have true access to our own mind, we can seek to understand other people's intentions. When teachers, administrators, or fellow students push your buttons, don't assume the worst. Utilize the four styles to examine why others act as they do. By looking at intentions based on style-driven needs and fears, you may just see others in a more positive light.

- REFRAME YOUR PERSPECTIVE and seek to understand the positive intentions of others.

- CONSIDER INTENTION prior to making judgments.

- DON'T IMPOSE YOUR INTENTIONS on others. Consider your own style as well as the style of the person with whom you are interacting.

- DON'T JUSTIFY POOR RESULTS or negative treatment of others with your positive intention.

Epilogue

The Journey Home

It was the first day of spring, and the sun had just risen over Home. A light fog floated on the forest floor as Xander stretched his neck to see above the hovering mist. Xenia and her apprentice were out for a morning walk. They saw new life piercing through the nurturing earth around them. The neighborhood trees bared hints of green, and the air smelled fresh and sweet.

As the chameleons walked side by side on the forest floor, Xenia shared stories of her younger days when she was learning how to adapt her appearance to the scenery. She told Xander of the time she attempted to match a raccoon and how, for two days, she looked as if she was wearing a mask.

Although Xander had improved on his ability to shift his color over the past year, he was still having a little difficulty matching rocky terrain.

"You're trying too hard," Xenia noted. "You're attempting to get the stones to adapt to you when, instead, you need to adapt to them."

"Well, it would be a lot easier if they just adapted to me," Xander said with the hint of a smile.

"If only it were that easy," Xenia replied.

"I know," Xander said. "The only thing I can truly change is myself."

They walked together up a slight incline and came across a family of unfamiliar doves enjoying their breakfast. Xander made eye contact with the mother dove, who immediately waved them up. The two chameleons scurried up the tree to join the group.

"Welcome, friends," the father dove said.

"Thank you for inviting us into your home," Xenia replied. "What a lovely crew you have here."

"Oh, thank you. We're quite proud of our little ones," the mother dove responded. "We've got plenty of food. You're welcome to stay for breakfast."

"Thank you so much," Xenia replied, "but don't worry about us. We're fine."

"Really, it's no trouble at all," the father dove said. "It would be our pleasure."

"I'd love to stay," Xenia acknowledged, "but I promised Xander's parents I wouldn't keep him out too long today. We really must be moving on."

"It won't take too long. And what kind of hosts would we be if we didn't feed you? Let me fix you both a little something," the mother dove insisted.

Xenia smiled and respectfully took the meal she was offered. She finished everything she was given. Xander, on the other hand, had recently eaten a large breakfast at home, and he wasn't hungry.

"Don't you like it?" the mother dove asked. "It's good for you. It will help you grow to become a big, strong chameleon like your teacher."

"I'm just not that hungry."

"How about one bite?" the dove encouraged.

Xander complied, and soon the two chameleons continued on their way with a satchel full of food in case they got hungry on their walk. The chameleons made their way past a field of large boulders when a young owl couple spotted them. The male called out, "Where are you going?"

"We're heading to the Great Lake to bring a message to my father," Xenia replied.

"Please tell him we send our regards," the female requested.

"Will do. How's your new tree hollow coming along?"

"Very well," replied the male owl.

"Not so good," countered his wife with a glare.

"Anything I can help you with?" the chameleon offered.

"No, thank you," said the husband. "We just cannot seem to agree on how to arrange the items in the hollow."

"That is because you are not following the plan," she replied.

"That is because your plan is not right," he retorted. "My plan is based on what I have been doing since I was Xander's age."

"Well, my parents taught me the right way to do this, and your way is not it," said the wife.

Xenia waved to the owls, who seemed lost in their conversation. She and Xander continued toward the lake. As they walked on, they could hear the owls continuing their debate until their voices faded into the distance.

As the chameleons approached the Great Lake, Xander spotted a blue flash out of the corner of his eye. A moment later, a green bolt of color whizzed by them so close that they could feel the wind from it on their faces. They quickly realized that the parrots were dive bombing the lake, trying to drop pine cones into a circle of twigs in the center of the water.

"Twenty points," the bright green parrot taunted. "Beat that!"

Just then a blue-and-yellow blur flew by, and another pine cone plummeted towards its target.

"Oh, so close," the green parrot announced.

"Hey, it's Xenia and her new little buddy," the blue parrot noted. "What's shakin'?"

"I'm looking for my father, Xavier. Have you seen him?" Xenia asked.

"Nope," replied the two parrots at the same time. "But hey," added the blue parrot, "we could use your help. We need someone to judge the competition. What do you say?"

"I'd love to help," the chameleon replied, "but I've got a message to deliver, and I need to get Xander back to his parents."

"It'll just take a few minutes," the green parrot pleaded. "We could sure use your help. And I bet that Xander will enjoy watching this."

The young chameleon glanced at his teacher. Seeing his eager eyes, she couldn't say no. "Alright, but just for a few minutes."

After several rounds of judging the target competition, Xenia and Xander thanked the parrots for letting them take part in their game and continued on their way. The pair was circling the outskirts of the lake when they noticed Xavier meditating on a large palm leaf set on a large boulder. His legs were crossed, and his palms rested peacefully on his lap. Without opening his eyes, he warmly greeted his visitors. After catching up for a few minutes,

Xenia delivered her message to her father. She didn't have much time to spend with the master chameleon because the doves, owls, and parrots had eaten up most of their extra time.

Father and daughter shared a few words, stared deeply into each other's eyes for a long moment, hugged, and parted. Then Xenia and Xander began retracing their steps back to Xander's parents. They were almost at Xander's home when he spotted an eagle circling high above. In a flash, the eagle swooped down and landed with a thud in front of the chameleons.

"Hello," the large eagle said.

"Good morning," Xenia replied.

"I noticed that you walked to the Great Lake and are now returning home," he noted.

"That's correct," Xenia confirmed.

"You didn't take the fastest route," the eagle commented.

"You are very observant," the chameleon acknowledged.

"Next time, take the lower pasture and head towards the Great Boulder. From there pass the Council Tree and head south to the Great Lake. That's the best route."

"Thank you so much," said the chameleon. "Your advice is much appreciated."

"You're welcome," the eagle stated. And with that, he was gone.

Xander turned towards the elder chameleon and said, "He seems to have a pretty strong idea about which is the best path to follow."

"Everyone does," Xenia replied.

"But it's more than that, isn't it?" Xander asked.

"Go on," Xenia requested.

"Since you've been teaching me, I have noticed that everyone imposes who they are on others. We saw that several times today."

"Even the doves?" Xenia asked knowingly.

"Even the doves," Xander smirked. "They offered us food that we didn't really want."

"Very observant. But it goes deeper than just imposing food. They imposed kindness. You see, they appreciate kindness from others, so they imposed kindness on us, even when we didn't want it."

"That makes a lot of sense," Xander said.

"Then, we saw the owls. What did they impose on us?"

"They didn't impose anything on us. They imposed on each other their ideas on how the tree hollow should be organized."

"Ah, the owls," Xenia reflected. "They often have such a clearly defined view of how things should be done that they impose their way on others."

Xander hopped over a small branch and said, "And you gotta love the parrots."

"What did they impose?"

"Well, they were just having fun, but they imposed that on us, too," Xander explained.

"You're right," Xenia confirmed. "They imposed on us their desire to play when we had a job to do."

Xander turned to watch several chipmunks scurrying up a tree, and then concluded, "And that brings us back to the eagle. He imposed his path on us. But I'm guessing it goes beyond that."

"Yes, it does," Xenia agreed. "Eagles often speak with such confidence and conviction that it's hard to say no to them, even if they are just sharing an opinion. They impose their ideas on others."

The two chameleons made their way back to Xander's home. Just before Xenia left him, she advised her young friend, "Remember, Xander, the secret to being a great chameleon is to adapt to others and not impose who you are on them."

He nodded a quick thank you.

Xenia smiled. Just before she faded into the lush green grass, she said, "You have returned home to where you began. But now you see with new eyes. You have grown much over this past year, and it is time for you to live what you have learned. Share what has been entrusted to you. It is time for you to take flight in every aspect of your life."

- The End -

Your Journey Begins

As I travel the world sharing the birds and the principles of *The Chameleon*, I am still struck by the impact the Eagle, Parrot, Dove and Owl have on people's lives. For nearly twenty years, I used letters (D, I, S, C) to symbolize each of the styles. I never could have imagined the degree to which people would connect to the birds. (Although admittedly, it is disconcerting that so many people want me to add "Vulture" to the list of bird personalities.)

In my days using letters, people usually asked questions about the traits of the four styles. Not anymore. Since the bird metaphor helps people learn the styles so easily, people quickly transition from grasping the styles to wanting tactics for using them on a daily basis.

When asked about applying the styles, I say that the first step after learning about the Eagle, Parrot, Dove and Owl is to know your own style. You have probably already accomplished this by reading *The Chameleon* and seeing yourself in the fables or if you like, you can complete the *Taking Flight with DISC* profile (available at TakeFlightLearning.com).

Once you know your style, the next step is to identify the styles of the people you meet. When you know yourself and others, you can treat people the way *they* need to be treated and not unwittingly impose your style on them.

Consider an Owl who inflicts too many household rules on his Parrot spouse. Or imagine a Dove grandmother who insists that visitors eat, even when they are not hungry. They both imposed their styles on others. Picture a Parrot who encourages his Dove friend to take part in a high-risk adventure when the Dove doesn't feel comfortable. And think of an Eagle parent who encourages an Owl child to take a leadership position on a school project when the child would rather play the role of researcher. They, too, imposed their styles on others.

Note that none of these individuals above had negative intentions. Nonetheless, they imposed their personalities on other people. They unconsciously assumed that others had the same needs and desires as they do. Without meaning to, they sent the message, "My way is the right way." Even worse, they conveyed, "Who you are is not okay."

Alternatively, when we honor the stylistic needs of others, we enable them to revel in their gifts and fulfill their deepest needs. If we respect the personality styles, we can build meaningful relationships throughout our lives.

Once people understand the importance of knowing and using the styles, the next question I often get is, "But how do I figure out someone's style if they haven't taken an assessment?"

This is easier than you might think. Look at body language, tone, rate of speech, intensity, level of risk-taking, decisiveness, and pace. These markers reveal someone's style. In fact, after reading

The Chameleon, you probably see Eagles, Parrots, Doves and Owls everywhere you go. From your server in a restaurant to a character on a television show to a coworker in the office, you are likely experiencing something called the Baader-Meinhof phenomenon. (Sorry about that.)

Ever notice that when you take up a new hobby like jogging, suddenly you see joggers everywhere? Or the day after you buy yourself a red convertible, you can't believe how many people drive red convertibles? This is Baader-Meinhof. Now that you have learned about the birds, you will likely see them in everyone you meet and especially in those who are closest to you.

Fortunately, identifying the styles of others is a skill. The more you practice it, the better you get at it. I challenge you to pay attention to the people around you and try to determine their styles. If you look for style, you will find it.

That said, the next question I often receive is, "But what if I can't figure them out? I've seen this person display different styles at different times."

Simple: you just need to determine which style he or she portrays *in that moment* and reflect it back. If the individual asks very specific questions, be the Owl and provide highly detailed answers. If the person speaks quickly and directly, be the Eagle and get right to the point. If responses are short on details and filled with enthusiasm, turn up the positive energy and be the Parrot. And if the individual conveys deep feelings, embody those emotions and connect with them as a Dove.

Since people tend to treat others how they themselves wish to be treated, use that to your advantage and reflect back what you observe. Or, as I like to say, *Be the Chameleon*. Adapt to how people treat you, and you will satisfy the needs they have in that moment.

At this point, the conversation often takes an interesting turn when I am asked, "Isn't it manipulative to be the chameleon?"

My answer is an emphatic, "No!"—with one caveat.

If your heart is pure and you truly want to help others, you honor people, not manipulate them. However, if you try to influence people to do something that will not serve them, then your intention is not pure and yes, that is manipulation.

To ensure that you are not manipulating others, set your intention to meet both your needs AND their needs. Being the chameleon does not mean accommodating others at every turn. That becomes a lose-win scenario in which they get what they want, but you don't. When you act as the chameleon, you find solutions that satisfy the needs of others *and* your needs as well.

Consider the Owl manager who adapts her style, providing few details and greater flexibility when delegating work to a Parrot. The Owl might just find that the Parrot does a great job and feels a high level of personal satisfaction. The Parrot may even improve the process.

Occasionally, this answer leads to a pointed question that addresses manipulation head on. A salesperson, for example, may ask me, "If I use the styles to try to make the sale, isn't that manipulation?"

By now, you can anticipate my answer. If you believe your product or service is right for the customers and in their best interest, it is your duty to help them see that. Flexing to a customer's style benefits him or her and, of course, you as a salesperson.

This is the point when I often encounter resistance, receiving two questions that sound something like, "But if I am adapting my style all of the time, aren't I being untrue to myself? And won't that be exhausting?"

My answers seem to surprise people: "Yes and yes." You do not need to *Be the Chameleon* in every moment of every interaction. That would be draining and ultimately self-defeating.

Instead, *Be the Chameleon* in important moments. When you find yourself in a critical conversation, it's a good time to adapt.

Remember, you honor yourself and demonstrate empathy when you act as the chameleon. If you want to raise well-balanced children, be in a mutually rewarding marriage, and work well with your coworkers, flexing to the needs of others is an act of compassion. But, it does take energy.

I will leave you with this thought: the most successful people are the most adaptable. Charles Darwin said, "It is not the strongest of the species that survives, nor the most intelligent that survives. It is the one that is most adaptable to change."

I'll take that one step further and say that the most adaptable people are also the happiest. Flexible people have less conflict and therefore less drama. They guide themselves to careers that play to their strengths and they cultivate relationships based on respect rather than judgment. Satisfying the needs of others is not about changing who you are, but rather honoring who they are. So, be yourself and whenever the situation calls for it, *Be the Chameleon!*

About the Author

MERRICK ROSENBERG is the CEO of Take Flight Learning. He is an accomplished entrepreneur, keynote speaker, facilitator and author. In 1991, he co-founded Team Builders Plus, which paved the way for team building as we know it. In addition to innovating more than a dozen team building programs, he led DISC personality styles training for more than 20,000 people. In 2012, Merrick went on to found Take Flight Learning to bring the four styles to the world in a more meaningful and impactful way.

Merrick is an engaging speaker who has shared his insights with many organizations such as TEDx, Association for Talent Development, Society for Human Resource Management, Project Management Institute and Vistage International.

Merrick has worked with small and mid-sized businesses as well as more than half of the Fortune 100 companies. Over the years, Merrick has shared his wisdom with organizations such as AAA, Adidas, Aramark, Bank of America, Blue Cross Blue Shield, Campbell Soup Company, Chase, Colgate Palmolive,

Comcast, ExxonMobil, Ford Motor Company, General Electric, GlaxoSmithKline, Hewlett-Packard, InterContinental Hotels Group, Johnson & Johnson, L'Oreal, Lockheed Martin, Lufthansa, Nabisco, National Institute of Health, NBCUniversal, Nestle Purina, Novartis, PECO Energy, Pepsi, Philadelphia Eagles, QVC, Roche, Samaritan Hospice, Temple University, UnitedHealthcare, Verizon and many more. Merrick has also led sessions for government agencies such as the Environmental Protection Agency, Homeland Security, Interpol, and the Social Security Administration, as well as the US Army, Navy, Air Force and Marines.

Merrick received his MBA from Drexel University, who selected him as their Alumni Entrepreneur of the Year. Under Merrick's leadership, his companies have received numerous awards including New Jersey Business of the Year by NJ Biz magazine, one of the Fastest Growing Companies in the U.S. by Inc. magazine, and on numerous occasions, one of the *Fastest Growing Companies* and *Best Places to Work* in the Philadelphia region by the Philadelphia Business Journal.

His first book, *Taking Flight!*, changed the way people think about personality styles.

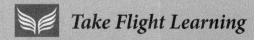 *Take Flight Learning*

Take Flight Learning reimagined the age-old DISC model by linking the four letters to visually appealing birds and providing a more brain-friendly and engaging approach to learning.

Take Flight Learning offers a variety of DISC training programs, products and services. The Taking Flight with DISC profile and workshop provide the foundation for understanding yourself and others. This groundbreaking session takes DISC training to new heights, as people learn to flexibly adapt to the people and situations in their lives. The Chameleon Leader and Chameleon Selling programs build on the Taking Flight with DISC session to transform leadership and selling skills.

Through a growing network of affiliates around the world, Take Flight Learning offers consultants the opportunity to grow their practice like never before. DISC certifications are available for consultants and in-house trainers who want to reinvent how to teach people about the styles.

Merrick Rosenberg is available as a keynote speaker to enliven conferences with DISC wit and wisdom.

Praise for The Chameleon

The lessons in this engaging book pack a powerful punch. With Rosenberg's remarkably perceptive insights, we can finally understand the particular forces that drive our behavior and interact with others more successfully than ever!
—**Marshall Goldsmith**, author of the *New York Times* and *Wallstreet Journal* #1 Best Seller *Triggers*

The Chameleon breathes life into the DISC behavioral styles by giving you characters and stories that you will see yourself in. More importantly it provides wisdom that you will hold onto, internalize and implement more than you ever could with your DISC profile alone.
—**Mark Goulston**, author *"Just Listen" Discover the Secret to Getting Through to Absolutely Anyone*

This book is filled with practical ways to build strong relationships and winning teams. Merrick Rosenberg has shown he's not just a great speaker, he's a great writer as well.
—**Ron Jaworski**, ESPN Analyst

Some will remember the fables; others will remember the lessons. But everyone will feel the impact of these powerful truths that can transform even the most challenging relationships. Every boss, every parent, every coach, every friend—read this!
—**Michael Wilkinson**, author of *The Secrets of Facilitation*

Through a series of cleverly written and relatable fables, *The Chameleon* brilliantly conveys the complexities and deepest truths of what it means to be human—living an authentic life, honoring and embracing the differences in others, and staying true to who we are yet learning how to adapt and change. Rosenberg masterfully combines his gift for storytelling with the depth of who he is as a teacher, business consultant and expert in human behavior.
—**Patricia Leuchten**, President and CEO, The Avoca Group

Merrick Rosenberg's collection of fables share timeless principles that challenge the way you think and act. *The Chameleon* is thought-provoking and transformational. This book should be required reading for anyone who pursues happiness and prosperity.
—**Vince Stango**, Chief Operating Officer, National Constitution Center

The Chameleon provides great insight into how to build prosperous relationships in business and in life. It will open your eyes to understanding different personalities and why it's important to treat others like they need to be treated vs. how you want to be treated.
—**Paul Muse**, President and Chief Executive Officer, 1st Advantage Federal Credit Union

If it's true that the most self-aware people are the most successful, those who read *The Chameleon* are destined for greatness. Rosenberg firmly establishes himself as a thought leader as he makes learning about yourself easy and enjoyable.
—**Sue Schick**, Chief Growth Officer, UnitedHealthcare

The chameleon wisdom contained in this book should serve as a valuable addition to any educator's collection—a true gem for teachers to understand themselves, their students and the dynamics in the classroom. Rosenberg captures the essence of how and why people get along and how they can create harmony, not just in school, but in any setting.
—**Salvatore J. Illuzzi**, Ph.D., Superintendent of Schools, Cinnaminson Township Public Schools

This book provides practical wisdom through captivating storytelling that is applicable and influential throughout the many aspects of your life. *The Chameleon* provides deep understanding of how the styles interact and how to get the most out of working together to fulfill your mission. Merrick's books continue to make me a better CEO, husband, and parent.
—**Kevin Havens**, CEO, Allied Health Media

When Merrick Rosenberg introduced the four bird styles to the world, I could never have imagined the impact they would have. *The Chameleon* teaches lessons about personality that help us to be the best we can be as we build enduring relationships and drive results. This is a book you should read, share and live.
—**Neil Aaron**, Senior Vice President, News Corporation

We have all learned the truism that "perception is reality." Merrick's engaging stories about eagles, parrots, doves, and owls teach us how our personality shapes our perceptions and how other peoples' personalities shape theirs. With this knowledge we can navigate past inaccurate perceptions and towards real communication and understanding. A great, instructive read.
—**Steve Johnson**, Rear Admiral, U.S. Navy (retired), Vistage Chair and Executive Coach

The Chameleon is a modern day Aesop's fables for people who deal with people, not only at work but in their personal lives as well. In each and every scenario, I was able to pick out the personality traits of co-workers, friends, family and myself. A great follow-up to Taking Flight with DISC and is now on my must read list for Leadership Development.
—**Terri Fanz-Falzone**, Sr. Human Resources Manager, TE Connectivity

Merrick Rosenberg has done it again. A few years ago, I discovered I was a strong eagle personality. That enabled me to adjust my behavior when interacting with doves, parrots and owls. Now, I am finding new insight as to how to be a chameleon. Powerful, practical and informative.
—**Gail Ruopp**, Executive Director, Flaster/Greenberg PC

As a CEO, I am always looking for ways to break down barriers to misunderstanding and improve communication throughout my organization. The fables in *The Chameleon* illustrate how understanding communication styles can help people connect

more effectively. I strongly encourage business leaders to introduce this book to their entire staff and tag along on an interesting journey through the forest.
—**Bob Rosania**, CEO, Ehmke Manufacturing Company

Merrick Rosenberg soars again with *The Chameleon* as his fables and bird styles teach us real-world applications helpful in both our personal and professional lives. This book is filled with sound advice for life-long learners of any age.
—**Michael Toscani**, Research Professor/Fellowship Director, Rutgers, The State University of New Jersey

In *The Chameleon*, Merrick Rosenberg uses his bird take on the DISC personality styles to teach readers about the different ways people work and communicate. His stories demonstrate how different personality types can go beyond just getting along to thriving together. Big props to Merrick!
—**Jay Scott**, Executive Director, Alex's Lemonade Stand Foundation

The Chameleon was a quick and easy read. I found it interesting how I related to different characters in different situations, which as a leader in my organization, reinforced my belief about inclusion and adaptation—getting the right people in the right seats and playing to people's strengths. This is not just a business book as its lessons apply in all aspects of our lives!
—**Rob Curley**, South Jersey President, TD Bank

Merrick Rosenberg's style is engaging and *The Chameleon* is a quick and easy read. The fables are practical and filled with real life situations you can relate to both personally and professionally. It's one of those books you can read over and over with a new takeaway each time. I highly recommend it.
—**Kristie Pappal**, Vice President of Human Resources, Philadelphia Eagles